The Oliver Wendell Holmes Lectures
are delivered annually at the Harvard Law School
under a fund established out of a legacy
to the Law School from Justice Holmes.
L. C. B. Gower was the Holmes lecturer
in November and December 1966.

Independent Africa

THE CHALLENGE TO THE LEGAL PROFESSION

L. C. B. Gower

Harvard University Press
CAMBRIDGE, MASSACHUSETTS
1967

Distributed in Great Britain by Oxford University Press, London

Library of Congress Catalog Card Number 67-20877

Printed in the United States of America

Preface

The chapters which follow were delivered in a slightly abbreviated form as four lectures in the Oliver Wendell Holmes series at the Law School of Harvard University on November 28, 29, and 30, and December 1, 1966. They should have been given early in 1965 but at the last minute had to be cancelled—to the great inconvenience of my hosts—since a dispute at Lagos University made it impossible for me to leave my post there. Harvard University insisted that the cancellation should be regarded only as a postponement and repeated their invitation for 1966. I am most grateful for this generosity and forbearance, and for the many kindnesses extended to me and my wife by the dean and other members of the Harvard law faculty during our stay in Cambridge.

The lectures are published in the form in which they were delivered and under the same title. Their scope is less extensive than that title might imply. They do not deal with the whole of independent Africa but only with sub-Saharan ex-British Africa, and principally with the countries of East and West Africa; a more accurate title might have been found but only by making it impossibly cumbersome. I must also emphasise that the lectures were prepared for oral delivery and though, I hope, reasonably adequate as such, are merely a series of impressionistic generalisations with no pretensions to deep scholarship. As such I would not have thought that they merited publication had not a number of those who heard the lectures urged the contrary.

I have tried to avoid technical jargon so far as possible. Terms such as "tribe" or "tribal" are not used in any precise anthropological sense; for my purposes "tribe" merely connotes one of several indigenous ethnic groups within each country, and friction between, say, the Hausas and Ibos of Nigeria is described as "tribal" in contrast with "racial" friction between white and black or African and Asian. However, I plead guilty to "anglophonic" and "francophonic" used as elegant variations for English-speaking and French-speaking. And no one talking about these parts of Africa can conveniently avoid "expatriate," about which a word of explanation may be desirable. It is an expression full of overtones (some pejorative, some euphemistic), connoting anyone—black or white—living in a country otherwise than as a native of it or, in general, as a permanent settler in it. In all the countries with which these lectures are primarily concerned (except Kenya) all "Europeans" (to use the African terminology) or "Caucasians" (to use the American) are, and were even prior to independence, expatriates in this sense. So are all non-Africans in West Africa. In relation to non-indigenous settler communities the usage is less clear cut. Already it seems that white settlers in Kenya have come to be regarded as expatriates, and it may be that before long the large Asian populations of East Africa will also be so regarded. At present an African from another part of tropical or southern Africa would not normally be described as an expatriate, but those from other parts of Africa (Egypt or Ethiopia) might be. Future usage in these respects will presumably depend on whether Pan-Africanism triumphs over nationalism or vice versa.

It is not easy for an expatriate to indulge in generalisations about African countries without appearing either unduly censorious or, what is worse, patronising or condescending. Judging from questions asked after the oral presentation of the lectures, some African readers will take exception, with their customary good humour, to some of my remarks; as will some British and American readers to my remarks concerning British and American policies and practices—which suggests that if I have offended I have at least done so without racial discrimination. I can only say that my intention was to provide both a frank criticism of the British colonial legacies to countries which I have come to love and admire and a sincere unsycophantic tribute to those who are now struggling with the problems flowing from these legacies. One interesting question is how far these problems are the same as those faced by countries with different (French or Belgian) colonial legacies or by countries (Ethiopia and Liberia) with no colonial legacy at all—but to deal with that would have needed another series of lectures.

I am deeply indebted to all those who have responded so generously to my requests for information or criticism. I refrain from naming the many African friends who have helped me because to do so might embarrass some of them. I must, however, express my sincerest thanks to Professor W. L. Twining, formerly of the Faculty of Law, University College of East Africa, Dar es Salaam; to Professor Robert B. Seidman, Mr. A. E. W. Park, and Mr. M. E. Naish, my former colleagues at the University of Lagos; to Professor S. A. de Smith; and to my wife, both for her customary patience with my customary irritability while in the throes of composition and for the illuminating accounts of her experiences as a teacher of English in West Africa. Needless to say, none of them bears any responsibility for the views which I have expressed. I am also most grateful to those who typed and retyped my many illegible manuscripts—Mrs. Julia Walters Duprée, Miss Barbara Warrington, and Miss P. A. Thorne.

London
March 1967

L. C. B. GOWER

Contents

Independent Africa

I

Pre-Independence: The Colonial Legacy

My object in these lectures is, first, to look at the legacies bequeathed by Britain, the former colonial power, to certain of the newly independent states of Africa; second, to assess what has happened to those legacies since independence, and what this means in terms of the legal profession; third, to consider whether these states presently have the legal professions that they need, and, if not, what is being done about it; and, finally, to ask what we in the West and in particular you in the United States can and should do to help. I shall concentrate on those countries which, until recently, were British dependencies and which received the mixed blessing of the common law and a judicial system in the Anglo-American tradition, and mainly on those in tropical Africa: Ghana, Nigeria, Sierra Leone, and the Gambia in the west; Kenya, Uganda, and Tanzania in the east.[1] We, as Anglo-American lawyers, are obviously in a better position to help them than the countries of

[1] Other common law countries to the south are Malawi (formerly Nyasaland), Zambia (formerly Northern Rhodesia), and to a lesser extent (because of the Roman-Dutch influence), the former High Commission Territories of Basutoland (now Lesotho), Bechuanaland (now Botswana) and Swaziland, and (not yet independent in the African sense of the term) Rhodesia and the Republic of South Africa.

French-speaking Africa, which have received the civil law. I ignore Liberia, the African country most influenced by the United States; I have never been there, and I want to speak, so far as possible, from first-hand experience only. If I appear to place disproportionate emphasis on Nigeria my reason is that it is there that I lived and worked for three years, and my excuse is that Nigeria is the largest and most populous of these countries and is, indeed, the most populous of all African countries; south of the Sahara one African in every four is a Nigerian. It is often said that where goes Nigeria so goes tropical Africa—a somewhat disturbing saying in the light of recent events.

It would, I am well aware, have been more scholarly if I had concentrated on one country only and made no statements about it unless they could have been fully documented. Instead, I shall indulge in generalisations, many of an essentially impressionistic character, most of which would require qualification if they were to be completely accurate in relation to any one country. These, however, are oral lectures, and were not prepared as a written work of scholarship.

First then, what are the legacies of British colonial rule? My first lecture is devoted to that question. In attempting to answer it I shall not try to draw up a balance sheet of the debits and credits of colonialism (there *are* credits as well as debits) but merely to refer to such items as seem to me to be particularly relevant to the legal profession. I must also make it clear that in framing my question as I have, I do not mean to suggest that the British must take the credit or the blame for everything that existed when these countries attained independence. On the contrary, the British contribution was merely a veneer on an indigenous political, cultural, and social structure. It was, however, a veneer that totally altered the appearance of most aspects of the basic structure which are of direct importance to the lawyer.[2]

If these legacies seem to be contradictory rather than coherent that, I suggest, is because British colonialism was contradictory in its aims. It was originally motivated by a forthright determination to exploit the colony for the benefit of the colonial power. Later that was overlaid, but never wholly obliterated, by higher aims and protestations: to spread Christianity, to eradicate the slave trade, to bear "the white man's burden," and finally to prepare the colonies for self-government. Some of the legacies are the product of one motive, some of the other, and some are hybrids of both. Contradictions are also inevitable because at present all these countries have two distinct societies whose problems cannot be solved by the same solution. The bulk of the population still live their traditional lives in a rural subsistence economy. A small but growing westernised minority live in the towns, much as we do in the West. Admittedly the latter retain contacts with the former. Nothing is more misleading than the common assumption that Africans can be clearly distinguished as rural tribesmen or detribalised urbanites. Thanks to the extended family system and clan and village unions that link the dwellers in the cities with their clansmen in the bush, no African is wholly detribalised. Nevertheless in all African countries there are two distinct societies to an

2 Indeed it did more than that. In the words of Barbara Ward, the West's colonial system "shook all the societies in the world loose from their old moorings." But, as she adds, we seem "indifferent whether or not they reach safe harbour in the end." Yet, in her words, "there is no human failure greater than to launch a profoundly important endeavour and then to leave it half done. This is what the West has done with its colonial system." *The Rich Nations and the Poor Nations* (London, 1962), p. 54.

extent unknown in Europe or North America, and a rule that is appropriate to one will probably be totally inappropriate to the other.

1. *Statehood*

The first legacy bequeathed to these countries is their existence as states. Like virtually all those in Africa, they owe their existence solely to the European Powers' scramble for colonies in Africa in the latter part of the nineteenth century. The territorial boundaries then carved out cut across all natural divisions—racial, tribal, and geographical. Within the boundaries of each is an infinite variety of peoples lacking any common culture, indigenous language, or religion. Nevertheless, the colonial powers succeeded in governing each as a separate entity, in imposing law and order within its boundaries, and in providing a *lingua franca*—English (pure or pidgin) in the case of the British colonies, and French in the case of most others. The newly independent African states may hate colonialism, but it was colonialism that gave them birth. By the time they were left to look after themselves they had become conscious of their national identities. On the other hand tribal loyalties remained stronger than national feelings, with the result that further fragmentation was a real risk. As most African states have populations of under five million, larger unions are clearly desirable and further fragmenting would be calamitous. Unhappily, colonialism had generated a sufficient feeling of nationhood to inhibit the former but not enough to prevent the latter.

2. *Membership of the Commonwealth*

The second legacy is membership in the Commonwealth. Except for Burma and the Sudan every British dependency which has achieved independence has elected to become a member of the Commonwealth—and only the Irish Republic and South Africa have since elected to leave it.[3] On the face of it this is surprising. While a country was a dependency the Commonwealth can have meant very little to it. It was at the best only a very junior member of the Commonwealth Club, denied any part in its management or the use of most of its amenities. The only facilities of much value to its people were Imperial Preferences—not of great importance to the African territories—and British nationality or the status of a British-protected person which, until the Commonwealth Immigrants Act in 1962, ensured free entry to the United Kingdom—though not to other countries of the Commonwealth. Moreover, large parts of the African territories were Protectorates or under Trusteeship and not British dominions at all. When such a territory is granted independence within the Commonwealth, with the Queen as head of state, it has then to be "annexed" to the Crown (as were the Northern Territories and Togoland in Ghana, the greater part of Nigeria and Sierra Leone, and the whole of Uganda and Tanganyika)—a curious adjunct to the grant of independence. Since a common allegiance to the Crown is no longer an essential element in Commonwealth membership, it would have been possible for these territories to have joined as republics (as Zambia has now done) and in view of the speed with which they embraced republicanism after independence it is strange that they did not. But even then they would have had to recognise the Queen as the symbolic head of the Com-

[3] Cyprus jumped from colonial status to independence outside the Commonwealth in August, 1960 but joined the Commonwealth in March, 1961.

monwealth, and a sentimental attachment to Her Majesty, such as is felt by British settlers in the older colonies, was totally absent. Furthermore, membership appeared to commit them to some extent to the Western bloc and therefore to run counter to their passionate desire to be "nonaligned."

Because of these considerations, it might have been expected that the African countries would have preferred to display their newly won independence by rejecting the colonial parent's nomination of them for membership in their club. That they did not is presumably due to their assessment of the tangible and intangible advantages which membership might confer—the hope of retaining British financial and technical assistance (France's reaction to Guinea's snub may not have been forgotten) and of being supported on their first appearance on the international stage by a group of powerful and friendly countries.[4] Certainly an impartial observer, at the time of independence, cannot have felt great confidence in the long-term survival of this particular legacy of British colonialism.

3. *The Legacy of Indirect Rule*

The policy of indirect rule laid down that the customs and traditions of the native populations should be interfered with as little as possible, and that the colonial power should exercise its authority through the traditional rulers. The path to self-government of these countries was, in the words of Lord Lugard (the author of the philosophy), to be "sought by the education of their own rulers and the gradual extension of their powers," rather

[4] These explanations may well be a rationalisation of what was really the automatic adherence to a pattern established by India and Pakistan.

than "by the introduction of an alien system of rule by British-educated and politically-minded progressives."[5] The appeal of this philosophy to the pragmatic unphilosophical British was that it lent an air of righteousness to colonialism—which they already suspected to be essentially unrighteous—and that its practice enabled colonies to be governed with the minimum of British money and manpower. Nor did it prevent the colonial power from getting its own way; a traditional ruler who failed to toe the line could be deposed and replaced—sometimes with scant regard for the traditional rules.[6] The traditional institutions were preserved but the traditional respect for them was undermined.[7]

In retrospect it is clear that this policy, and especially that aspect of it which excluded from the seats of power "British-educated and politically-minded progressives," had little chance of long-term survival except in the Fulani Emirates of Northern Nigeria, for which Lugard had originally enunciated it. This, indeed, was increasingly recognised—not least by Lugard himself. Nevertheless, it remained the *de facto* practice throughout British tropical Africa almost until the Second World War. In Kenya and the Rhodesias (white as opposed to

5 F. D. Lugard, *The Dual Mandate in British Tropical Africa*, 5th ed. (London, 1965), p. 86. Elsewhere he wrote: "It is a cardinal principle of British Colonial policy that the interests of a large native population shall not be subject to the will either of a small European class or of a small minority of educated and Europeanised natives who have nothing in common with them, and whose interests are often opposed to theirs." *Report on the Amalgamation of Southern and Northern Nigeria 1912-1919*, Cmd. 468, para. 40.

6 See, for example, *Eshugbayi Eleko* v. *Government of Nigeria* [1931], A.C. 662, P.C. On the other hand the colonial government's recognition of a chief made it more difficult for his subjects to remove him by the traditional processes and thereby diminished the democratic element in African life.

7 For a short account of this in the Gold Coast, see W. B. Harvey, *Law and Social Change in Ghana* (Princeton, 1966), chap. ii.

black Africa) the basic assumptions were somewhat modified, for there it was envisaged that in due course power would be handed over not to Africans at all but to the white minority. This, needless to say, led to even less association of "British-educated and politically-minded [African] progressives" in the processes of government.

This underlying philosophy has had long-term consequences which are still all-pervasive. In Northern Nigeria and the kingdoms of Uganda it entrenched the less progressive feudal overlords. Everywhere it helped to preserve rather than to break down tribalism, and to maintain divergent customary laws and the traditional tribunals which enforced them. It accentuated the rift between white rulers and black subjects and thereby pandered to the colour prejudice to which, unhappily, the Anglo-Saxon races seem particularly prone. It justified the use of "pidgin" or "kitchen" English as a means of communication during the temporary period of British suzerainty, and it affected the type and standards of education which were regarded as appropriate. It would do a grave injustice to the dedicated men and women who ran the mission schools to suggest that they deliberately inculcated something akin to "Bantu-education"—that most revolting feature of South African apartheid. But all too often the results were not dissimilar.

France, the other main colonial power, adopted a very different policy. She had no doubt of the superior virtues of French civilisation, law, and culture and regarded it as her mission to extend them as widely as possible in replacement of indigenous customs and institutions. She destroyed the powers of indigenous rulers. She sought to educate and assimilate her colonial subjects so that they were indistinguishable, except in colour (and the Latins are less colour-conscious), from Frenchmen.[8] With those Africans, admittedly all too few, who succeeded in obtaining a French education she succeeded to an astonishing extent.

The consequences of the British policy would have mattered less if the assumptions on which indirect rule was based had been fulfilled. In fact, however, these territories have not been left with a system of government based on their traditional institutions but with "an alien system of rule" based on the British. And those who now operate that system are not the traditional rulers but precisely those "British-educated [or American-educated] and politically-minded progressives" who had hitherto been cold-shouldered.[9] It was they who led the nationalist movements in the various countries and to whom power was handed over. After the Second World War, autocratic government through traditional rulers was superseded with varying degrees of rapidity by representative government both at the central and local government levels. In the realm of local government not very successful attempts were made to produce an amalgam of traditional authorities and representative local councils on the British model. At the centre, however, a totally "alien system of rule"—parliamentary democracy on the Westminster model—was installed by the time that independence was granted.

8 Dean Erwin N. Griswold of the Harvard Law School has recently pointed out that the difference may be partly due to the different attitudes of the civil and the common law. The former recognised the slave as a person; the common law did not recognise him at all but allowed him to be treated as a chattel. See Griswold, *Law and Lawyers in the United States* (London, 1964), pp. 105-107.

9 This statement requires some qualification in the case of Northern Nigeria and parts of Uganda where the traditional rulers still maintain some power.

It is indicative of the *volte-face* that has occurred that power was granted to African nationalists not only in black Africa but also in white Africa where we now decline to grant it to the white minority. The problem in Rhodesia is that too much power had been surrendered before the change of heart occurred.

4. *British-Style Education*

Before discussing the "Westminster model," I want to say a word about another related legacy of British colonialism, the educational system. Britain left her former African colonies with an embryonic educational system modelled closely on her own. So long as the policy of indirect rule was followed, African education[10] was largely in the hands of Christian missions, whose aim was primarily to convert to Christianity, to eradicate slavery and witchcraft, and to confer on their converts such an education as would fit them for the station in life to which it had pleased God to call them. Since, in the main the missions in British Africa had their headquarters in England or Scotland, the education which they gave was based on British ideas, except that it stopped short of the standards aimed at in Britain.[11]

The Christianity imparted was often only skin-deep and has not, in fact, withstood the spread of Islam, or, as yet, eradicated belief in witchcraft and juju. But the education was valued and has stuck. Those who achieved it were not content with what they could acquire locally

10 In East Africa, African education was segregated from Asian education, and both were segregated from European education.

11 There were, of course, exceptions such as the Catholics (whose missionaries, however, were predominantly Irish) and the famous Basel Mission whose trading wing still survives in West Africa as the powerful U.T.C. In Northern Nigeria it was part of Lugard's bargain with the emirs that there should not be any mission schools; the backwardness of education there is the direct result of this bargain.

and sought to further it by going abroad. Thereby not only did they achieve a fully Westernised education equivalent to that of their colonial masters but also the social cachet of the "been-to."[12]

When after the war indirect rule was scrapped, the colonial governments for the first time moved into the educational field in a big way. They set up new schools and assumed the major share of the finance and control of the policy of mission schools. They increased the facilities for higher technical education, and made a cautious start in local university education; it was excessively cautious, for until independence there were only four university colleges in British West and East Africa—Fourah Bay in Sierra Leone, in special relationship with the University of Durham, and Legon in Ghana, Ibadan in Nigeria, and Makerere in Uganda, all in special relationship with the University of London. All except Fourah Bay were of recent creation and in all cases their student numbers were small—far less than those who went abroad for a university career.

The general organisation, both of schools and universities, was on the British pattern. Children at secondary schools were required to take English school-leaving examinations—the Cambridge Overseas School Certificate in the case of those who were the brightest academically, and the examinations of the Royal Society of Arts and the like in the case of the others.[13] The belief, justified in the early days, was that any such qualification would open the door to white-collar employment, which

12 A West African expression unknown in East Africa—probably because so few East Africans were given the opportunity of "going to."

13 In the early 1920's the colonial government in Nigeria wanted to introduce a Nigerian School Certificate instead. The idea had to be dropped in the face of an outcry based on the assumption that the local examination would be inferior.

alone was highly prized. A classical education was especially valued, and far more African children learned Latin and Greek than French.

The university colleges, allied as they were to English universities, taught for English degrees. Although their "special relationship" arrangements allowed for adaptation to local conditions, not much use was made of this freedom since the teachers were largely British and tended to believe in the syllabuses and curricula with which they were familiar. Facilities at the universities were lavish—in the "Oxbridge" rather than the "redbrick" tradition. But it was the Oxbridge apparatus rather than its essence which was imported. Chapels, libraries, commonrooms, and music rooms were built; academic gowns were worn and Latin graces intoned from High Tables. But a highly educated student body from an exceptionally cultured home background was not available and without it the tutorial or supervision system, which is the essence of Oxbridge's instruction, could not function properly. The emphasis tended to be on the traditional academic disciplines rather than on technological or vocational training—English history and literature, the classics and philosophy, rather than medicine, law, engineering or agriculture. Since the teaching faculty consisted almost exclusively of British expatriates, academic salaries were tied to British scales and frequent home leave was granted during the very long vacations. Those who raised their voices against the creation of academic ivory towers, producing an intellectual elite remote from their own people, were decried as displaying the outmoded colonial belief that the best was too good for the Africans.[14]

The criticism of the educational legacy must be that

[14] See also the incident referred to in n.13.

which can be levelled against so many British activities —we did too little, we did it too late, and we made insufficient adjustment to local conditions. On the other hand, the French made fewer adjustments still, and in comparison with them, we gave some sort of education to a relatively large proportion of our colonial people; and we left them with a thirst for more.[15] Perhaps the gravest defect of English education was, surprisingly, in the teaching of the English language, and it is here that the contrasts with French-speaking Africa are most striking. A highly educated African from francophonic Africa speaks like a Frenchman, thinks like a Frenchman, and indeed, still often regards himself as a Frenchman first and an African second.[16] With rare exceptions, an African from anglophonic Africa (especially West Africa) does not speak or think like an Englishman.[17]

Most English-speaking Africans would say that they do not want to be black Englishmen or to write and speak English like Englishmen—you, I am sure, will sympathise with them. The fact is, however, that throughout the former British territories of West and East Africa English remains the official language, the language of the law, and the *lingua franca* of everyday communication. In East Africa, Swahili[18] may one day replace it, but in West Africa there is no indigenous

15 The Belgians were conspicuously successful (though they now get little credit for it) in the training of artisans but had made very little progress in higher education.

16 The quest for "negritude" (a concept which has little appeal in "British" Africa) is the intellectual's emotional reaction to this assimilation.

17 And, incidentally, he regards himself first as a Hausa, Ibo, Yoruba, Kikuyu (or whatever his ethnic group is), second, as a national of his country, third, as an African, and as an Englishman not at all.

18 It is already the *official* language for government business in Zanzibar except in the superior courts and an alternative official language in the Tanganyikan National Assembly.

language that could. Those who now govern these countries and make or administer their laws will be immensely handicapped unless they can think and write in English with clarity and precision.[19] So long as that is so, by all means let African-English diverge from British-English in idiom, intonation, pronunciation, and even vocabulary, just as American-English does. But, at present, English, as spoken and written by most educated Africans, including many of those in the highest positions, is not a sufficiently precise instrument.[20]

5. *The Westminster Model*

The fifth major legacy of colonial rule was the Westminster model of parliamentary democracy. Representative legislatures elected, in most cases, on the principle of one man (and one woman), one vote, had been set up during the short era of internal self-government which preceded full independence. Rival political parties, it was assumed, would fight the elections and a government would be formed by the winning party. Its leader would become prime minister and choose his cabinet from among the elected members of his party. They would form "Her Majesty's Government" in the territory and would be collectively responsible to parliament for their actions. The role of the largest losing party would be to provide "Her Majesty's Loyal Opposition" with a shadow cabinet ready to take over the reins of government in due course. In the meantime

19 And read it much more rapidly than most do at present.

20 There are, of course, wide variations in standards. A few schools have a deserved reputation for producing admirable English-speakers and some Africans who have been educated abroad speak it perfectly. Standards are higher in East Africa than in West Africa, and higher in Sierra Leone than elsewhere in West Africa, due, presumably, to the influence of those who returned from slavery.

they would oppose and criticise the government with decorum and restraint, seeking to swing the pendulum of public opinion in their favour and to defeat the government party and gain power, but only by the constitutional processes of reasoned argument and the ballot-box.

On paper the independence constitutions of the former British colonies in West and East Africa followed the Westminster model in almost every detail. They differed from the British model in form, of course, because the British constitution is unwritten and based largely on observed, but not legally enforceable, conventions. In contrast, the constitutions of the newly independent African states were embodied in legislation,[21] and the constitutional conventions were spelled out in some detail. In some cases too, there were inevitable differences of substance; Nigeria, Kenya, and Uganda, had been federalised and to that extent necessarily diverged from the unitary Westminster model.[22] The peculiar position of Buganda and its traditional ruler and legislature, the Kabaka and the Lukiko, led to differences in the constitution of Uganda. But in general, so far as political organisation is concerned, the African territories of West and East Africa were left with the Westminster model, pure and simple—or rather pure but far from simple.

21 In a (U.K.) Order in Council. Independence itself was conferred by a (U.K.) statute. Not unnaturally the newly independent states disliked these reminders that legally they owed their independence to acts of their colonial masters, and the speed with which the independence constitutions were followed by republican ones was due as much to a desire to have truly autochthonous constitutions as to any dislike of the monarchy.

22 They were federations of an unusual type in that they represented not a coming together of separate states but a breaking-up of unitary systems in response to pressure from below.

Britain is sometimes criticised for, it is alleged, imposing her own strange brand of parliamentary democracy on her former colonies. In fact, however, the evidence is clear that she did no such thing, but that the former dependencies voluntarily chose it.[23] As Professor de Smith puts it, the Westminster model "has been the most sought after of Britain's exports to the Commonwealth. . . . It has been demanded partly because it is familiar to colonial politicians, partly because they genuinely admire the way in which it works in Britain, partly because they have sometimes been told that they lack the political maturity to operate it effectively, partly because it makes for very strong government if a single party is dominant."[24]

To these reasons one more can be added: ex-colonies seem to feel that they cannot be sure that they have won their freedom unless they can exercise it in the same garments as those worn by their former masters. Later they may design their own clothes, but first they must don those of the colonialists. To quote de Smith again: "Colonial politicians have often asserted that they need a constitution designed to meet the special problems of their own country; yet modifications of the Westminster model that might have rendered it more adaptable to local conditions have been viewed with suspicion. The last voice to incant the slogan "British is Best" is likely to be that of a colonial nationalist. . . ."[25] Doubtless in some instances there was the realisation that the choice of the Westminster model familiar to the constitution-

23 That they could have had a different sort of constitution if they had wanted it is shown by the example of Zambia, which asked for and got an independence constitution not on the Westminster model.

24 S. A. de Smith, *The New Commonwealth and Its Constitutions* (London, 1964), p. 68.

25 *Ibid.*

makers in London would avoid delay in the march to independence.[26] But only to that extent were Britain's views of any moment; the former colonies got the Westminster model because they wanted it, not because Britain wanted them to have it—though doubtless she did.

Whether they were wise to want it is another question. It works reasonably well in Britain, but there has been remarkably little research to find out what it is in Britain's social and economic conditions which accounts for its success. When a crop grows well it follows that the soil and climate are right and there is no particular need to ask why. But if one is proposing to sow the seed elsewhere an obvious first step is to carry out a careful survey of the soil and climate of both countries. The delicate seed of parliamentary democracy was planted in Africa without any such survey.[27] Another obvious precaution is a long period of controlled sowings. This did not happen either. Tanganyika, for example, got the Westminster model much as she got her ill-fated Groundnut Scheme—in haste and on a grand scale. In 1958 she held her first parliamentary elections of any sort, and in 1961 she became independent as a parliamentary democracy. We are apt to criticise France and Belgium for the speed of their withdrawal and the inadequate period of preparation for independence and democratic government which they allowed their colonies; but they were not unique in these respects.

No sensible person, I think, can have expected that parliamentary democracy would work in Africa as it

26 *Ibid.*, p. 69.

27 For this point, and the metaphor in which it is clothed, I am indebted to Professor W. A. Robson: see "Transplanting of Political Institutions and Ideas" (1964) 35 *Political Quarterly* 407.

does at Westminster. The most that could have been hoped was that it would adapt itself to novel conditions and survive as an acceptable variation of the British plant. Even that was unlikely.

6. *The Civil Service Tradition: The Whitehall Model*

The sixth legacy which Britain bequeathed was a public service which was reasonably efficient and fair, and free of the corruption and nepotism which are endemic in Africa and most other continents. Unhappily, while the policy of indirect rule prevailed, the public service of the colonial power was tiny and, at the administrative and professional levels, almost exclusively expatriate. That policy was scrapped far too late to build up a service of adequate size and with a sufficient mixture at all levels of expatriates and Africans so that the experienced expatriates could train the Africans and instil in them the high traditions of the British Civil Service. Until after independence the service remained incredibly small for the administration of a modern state, with the British at the top, Africans at the bottom, and, in East Africa, Asians in the middle. Africanisation had proceeded further in West Africa than in East; but in 1959 on the eve of independence in Nigeria, and after something approaching a crash programme of Nigerianisation in the Federal Public Service, Nigerians held only one out of fourteen posts of permanent secretary, two out of twenty posts of deputy permanent secretary, and six out of thirty-four posts of senior assistant secretary.[28]

[28] Out of a total of seventy-three super-scale posts in the administrative service, West Africans held only ten. See the *Final Report of the Parliamentary Committee on the Nigerianisation of the Federal Public Service: Session Paper 6 of 1959* (Lagos, 1959), quoted in Robert O. Tilman and Taylor Cole (eds.), *The Nigerian Political Scene* (Durham, N.C., 1962), p. 104.

The same pattern extended throughout the whole range of the service, including the judiciary and the police. There was a small cadre of expatriates at the top of an inadequate African infra-structure. Except in Ghana, Nigeria, and Sierra Leone, no start had been made on the Africanisation of the judiciary or magistracy. Indeed, until shortly before independence no clear distinction was drawn between administrative and magisterial functions—the latter as well as the former being undertaken by expatriate officers without legal qualifications. Moreover, until the introduction of internal self-government, there was little opportunity to instil the fundamental principle that politicians determined policy and non-political civil servants carried it out. The colonial power might, and did, forbid its African civil servants from playing an active part in politics, but the officers of the colonial service clearly determined policy as well as executed it.

A civil service on the British model was therefore a small newborn baby when independence came. All the independence constitutions contained provisions which it was hoped would ensure that it was reared on traditional British lines. The appointment, transfer, promotion, discipline, and dismissal of public officers were vested in an independent public service commission, whose members enjoyed security of tenure and who themselves could not be public servants or members of parliament. Thereby it was hoped to protect the public service from the canker of corruption and nepotism, to insulate it from political patronage or victimisation, and to ensure that the relationship between minister and officials should be based as closely as possible on the Whitehall model—the essential administrative adjunct to the Westminster model.

7. *The Military and the Police*

I confess that when I originally prepared these lectures two years ago it did not occur to me to make specific mention of the military as one of the important legacies of colonial rule relevant to my theme. In view of recent events a brief word about the military as well as the police seems to be necessary.

Upon independence the former colonies were left with small, very small, regular armies organised and trained on British lines and armed with British weapons. Originally the officers were exclusively British but during and after the Second World War a few Africans were commissioned, and efforts, surprisingly successful, were made to steep them, too, in the Sandhurst tradition. Up to independence, however, the senior officers were still British.

In the case of the much larger police forces the curious constitution of the British domestic product did not provide an organisational model that could be followed.[29] But an attempt could be, and was, made to reproduce something of the British spirit. As in Britain the police were unarmed and were treated as a law-enforcement, crime-detecting, and traffic-controlling agency, and not as a para-military body. Under the supervision of British officers, many of whom were formerly in the British police forces, they were trained in the British manner and in British police methods. As with the army, a cautious start on the Africanisation of the officer corps was made prior to independence.

29 "There is no prospect of reproducing in any country overseas the peculiar constitutional status of the British police—a collection of semi-autonomous local forces commanded by Chief Constables (surely the most singular of constitutional anomalies) with central and local government authorities exercising a hotch-potch of executive and supervisory functions." de Smith, *New Commonwealth*, pp. 150-51.

Hence the Sandhurst-model army was to some extent matched by the New Scotland Yard-model police. But in colonial days the police, like the military, were inevitably regarded as the agents of the alien ruling power. This made it impossible to reproduce the friendly image of the British "bobby" whom you Americans traditionally think of as "wonderful" and to whom we British traditionally turn for help.

With the grant of independence it was recognised that something should be done to prevent the police from becoming, or from being regarded, as the instrument of the party in power. In particular it was vital to prevent recruitment, promotion, and disciplinary control from being dominated by partisan considerations. Hence the independence constitutions provided for police service commissions, analogous to, and in some cases merged in, the public service commissions. Sometimes, too, the inspector general (the police head) was accorded a semi-autonomous status. In Nigeria the police were made a federal responsibility—but without, unfortunately, banning regional forces as well.

The hope was that both the army and the police would maintain the impartial non-political traditions of their British counterparts. Total insulation of operational control from political direction was obviously neither desirable nor possible. But their primary domestic role was to be the maintenance of law and order without favouring any party or tribe; only thus could the Westminster model work properly by producing a government and parliament which would genuinely reflect the popular will. In countries where politicians had already begun to surround themselves by party thugs this role was obviously vital. It goes without saying that the last thing that was wanted was that they themselves should play politics—either on their own behalf or as the tools of others. What was hoped for was the rule of law, not the rule of force.

8. *The Rule of Law*

My eighth legacy is the rule of law. I am not going to attempt a definition of this; you will all have your own ideas of what it means and those ideas will have enough precision and similarity for my purposes. You will all agree, I imagine, that it implies respect for the individual's human rights. In Britain, however, this depends largely on enlightened public opinion and the tradition of centuries. There are no legal restraints on the sovereignty of parliament and we have no bill of rights. In the very different circumstances of tropical Africa it was agreed that something more was needed. Some steps in that direction were taken in the independence constitution of the first African state to throw off the colonial yoke—the Gold Coast, or Ghana as it became. But friction between the government and opposition parties, and the embarrassment which that caused to the British government, then inhibited much in the way of novel constitutional experiments.[30] It was left to Nigeria, which achieved independence three years later in an atmosphere of unusual harmony, to provide the pattern which was closely followed later both in Africa and elsewhere.

It would be brash indeed to suggest to an American audience that there is anything particularly novel in a legally enforceable bill of rights, such as was incorporated into the Nigerian constitution. But in the context

30 All the parties had expressed a desire to have incorporated a comprehensive code of fundamental rights but this would have involved more alterations to the existing constitution than the British government was prepared to embark upon in the circumstances.

of British-made constitutions it was a major breakthrough. Ironically, much of the credit for it is due to the Council of Europe, which thereby made a greater impact on Africa than it ever did on Europe. The Council had drafted a Convention of Human Rights designed to give legally enforceable effect to the aspirations expressed in the Universal Declaration of Human Rights. The United Kingdom not only ratified it but, rather surprisingly, extended it to forty-two of her dependencies, including all those in Africa except (alas!) Southern Rhodesia.[31] (France pointedly refrained from adopting or extending it to hers.) When Nigeria became independent she incorporated this convention, with minor amendments only, into her constitution, thereby making it an entrenched part of her domestic law.

The main reason for this incorporation was the need to placate the fears of her many racial minorities. But the fact that a newly independent African state had voluntarily subjected herself to restraints on her newly won legislative and executive sovereignty created a most favourable impression in the West. Contrasts were drawn, as they were meant to be drawn, with Ghana, which had already disappointed expectations by resorting to preventive detention and by embarking on constitutional amendments of an increasingly authoritarian character. Nigeria showed the world that while she may have attained independence later than Ghana she was not only much bigger but also much better. This initial impression stood her in good stead and is one of the reasons for the favourable press which she continued to enjoy, despite later events which might have been expected to shatter confidence in the belief that she was a model democracy.

31 See Cmd. 9045 of 1953.

With the exception of Tanganyika, all the former British territories which later attained independence started with enforceable bills of rights. To describe this as a legacy of colonialism is perhaps incorrect; at the most it was a *donatio mortis causa* made only in expectation of the immediate demise of colonial power. More accurately it was a family arrangement by the successors of colonialism. But at least it can be claimed that Britain has a tradition of respect for human rights which, by and large, she extended to the citizens of her empire so far as that was possible under conditions of enforced and increasingly unwelcome colonial rule. In particular, she allowed the nationalist movements a considerable measure of press freedom of which they made good use in building up their power and in hastening the departure of their colonial masters. This tradition Britain passed on, and the newly independent states sanctified it in legislation.

Respect for the rule of law, however, involves something more than a legally enforceable bill of rights (and can exist in its absence). Its essence, perhaps, is acceptance of the idea that however politically charged an issue may be, legal processes have a part to play and should be observed; that constitutional changes should be effected by the proper legal procedure; and that it is ultimately for the courts to determine whether that procedure has been observed. This idea, too, had been instilled and was bequeathed.[32] But it was thought that it would be a valueless legacy unless the judicial bench

32 For two recent examples of submission to the English courts of highly charged political issues, concerning Sierra Leone and the Gambia, see *Buck v. Attorney General* [1965] Ch. 745 C.A., and *Sabally and N'Jie* v. *Attorney General* [1965] 1Q.B. 273 C.A. Unfortunately the latter also shows that judicial decisions can be nullified by retroactive legislation—a lesson not lost on the new governments.

remained insulated from political interference. In Britain this insulation too depends very largely on tradition and convention. In law, judges are appointed by the executive and dismissible on an address by both houses of the legislature.[33]

In most of the colonies, judges were in theory dismissible merely at the pleasure of the Crown.[34] Accordingly, here again, greater safeguards were introduced. The independence constitutions (including those of Ghana and Tanganyika) vested judicial appointments, except that of chief justice, in an independent judicial service commission under the chairmanship of the chief justice with majority representation of the bench.[35] Dismissal of a judge involved an elaborate procedure of complaint, judicial investigation, and report, followed, if the report was adverse to the judge concerned, by reference to the Judicial Committee of the Privy Council. Attempts were also made to insulate criminal prosecutions from political interference by making the director of public prosecutions an independent officer with security of tenure, not subject to directions from the minister of justice or the cabinet. In other words, real efforts were made to make the rule of law a legal norm and not just a pious aspiration.

33 It has been well said that "In England judicial independence is maintained in spite of rather than because of the rules governing appointments." de Smith, *New Commonwealth*, p. 137.

34 See *Terrell* v. *Secretary of State for the Colonies* [1953] 2 Q.B. 482. But also see Kenneth Roberts-Wray, "The Independence of the Judiciary in Commonwealth Countries," in J. N. D. Anderson (ed.), *Changing Law in Developing Countries* (London, 1963), pp. 63-80; and Roberts-Wray, *Commonwealth and Colonial Law* (London, 1966), pp. 496-505.

35 Ghana also excluded justices of appeal. As Roberts-Wray points out, the exclusion of the chief justice was regarded as inevitable "since a body which makes recommendations for the appointment of persons to any public office cannot properly include persons who may be candidates." *Changing Law in Developing Countries,"* p. 66.

9. *The Common Law Legacy*[36]

The ninth legacy is that of the common law. The first point to stress here, however, is that English law was never imposed on these colonies in such a way as to oust the indigenous customary laws—that would have conflicted with the basic tenets of indirect rule. In this respect British policy was more realistic than that of the French. It recognised the existence of two separate societies and the fact that the subsistence sector must continue to be controlled by the norms of customary law. Hence in transactions between the indigenous population the relevant customary law normally continued to govern and would be applied by untrained judges in the traditional customary courts.[37] In general, these customary laws are unwritten and vary from area to area, race to race, and tribe to tribe. In some places, however, there is a more developed and generalised body of rules with a considerable literature—Islamic law—and the Alkalai judges who administer the *sharia* courts have had a legal training of a sort.[38]

Customary laws ceased to operate only to the extent that they were inconsistent with local legislation, or contrary to "natural justice, equity, and good conscience" or some such formula (a formula that at times has been given a wide interpretation but which latterly was normally restricted to customs that can fairly be regarded as barbarous). English law applied where cus-

36 For a more detailed discussion of the rules dealt with in this section, see A. E. W. Park, *The Sources of Nigerian Law* (London, 1963). Though directed to the position in Nigeria, its description is generally applicable to all the ex-British colonies in Africa.

37 Though latterly these derived their authority from local statutes, and to that extent ceased to be purely traditional.

38 To equate Islamic law with other customary laws is an over-simplification. In some countries its interrelation with other laws is less clear-cut than I have implied.

tomary law was inapplicable—for example, in transactions between expatriates or where the nature of the transactions between natives showed an intention to oust customary law. And English law for this purpose meant "the common law, the doctrines of equity and the statutes of general application which were in force in England. . ." on a particular cut-off date (1874 in the case of Ghana, 1897 in the case of Kenya, 1900 in the case of Nigeria, 1920 in the case of Tanganyika, and so on). Some of the local statutes thus providing for this reception of English law made it clear that the cut-off date applied only to statutes. Most did not, thus giving rise to the argument that English decisions handed down after the cut-off date should be ignored. Happily this absurdity was ignored in practice and the courts continued, perhaps too slavishly, to follow English decisions. "Statutes of general application" were nowhere defined, and no one, therefore, was quite sure which English statutes applied and which did not. If applicable, however, they did so only so far as local circumstances permitted and with such verbal alterations as might be requisite.[39]

These sources of law were further supplemented by local legislation and, indeed, by British legislation subsequent to the cut-off date if it expressly applied to the colony. In general, local legislation was unimaginative—a verbatim repetition of English legislation on the same subject matter. If, for example, a colony needed a Busi-

39 In some countries there was a similar power to apply common law and equity "subject to such qualifications as local circumstances may render necessary," and it has been argued that all the courts have an inherent power in similar terms by virtue of their general duty to administer justice; see Antony Allott, *Essays in African Law* (London, 1960), p. 25. In fact, however, little use has been made of this express power and less of the implied power if it exists.

ness Corporations Act, the Colonial Office would despatch a copy of the latest English Companies Act and it would be re-enacted in the colony without any consideration of whether it was really appropriate to local conditions. Thus in West Africa, Ghana's Companies Act was the English Act of 1862, Nigeria's that of 1908, Sierra Leone's that of 1929, and only the Gambia, the least developed and therefore the last to ask for legislation, had the latest English Act of 1948.[40] Occasionally, notably in the field of criminal law, an attempt was made to improve on England by producing a code. But these codes, too, were basically a restatement of English law at second hand through the Indian or Queensland Criminal Codes. Sometimes legislation by reference was resorted to; in most colonies, for example, matrimonial jurisdiction was to be exercised in accordance with the law and practice prevailing in England from time to time. In parts of East Africa, Indian statutes were made to apply.

The received law and local statutes were administered by British-type courts presided over by judges drawn from the Colonial Legal Service, and operating under a procedure based on that prevailing in the English courts but with the substitution, generally, of assessors or a judge alone for the jury.[41] At the apex of the judicial hierarchy there was a Court of Appeal for West Africa (now defunct) and another for East Africa (which still survives) and thence, with leave, an ultimate appeal to the Judicial Committee of the Privy Council in Lon-

40 In East Africa a uniform Companies Act was enacted in 1958 by Kenya, Uganda, and Tanganyika. This was the first serious attempt to improve upon the English model and to adapt it to local conditions. It has not yet been brought into operation in Tanganyika.

41 Operating, moreover, with all the paraphernalia of English tradition, including wigs and gowns, totally unsuited to tropical conditions.

don. In general, customary courts were prohibited from administering the received law or local legislation. But the British courts could administer customary law when it was applicable to a dispute before them, though in that event it had to be proved as a fact. Increasingly, too, supervision over the customary courts was exercised by appeal to, or review by, the British courts, and by a system of inspection by trained lawyers. Before independence the customary courts had, therefore, been integrated to a greater or lesser degree into a common court system, and, everywhere, efforts were being made to ensure that all judges received some sort of training.

It will be seen that the legal legacy was one of extreme complication, fraught with problems of internal conflicts between diverse customary laws and between customary laws and the received law. English law was applied without consideration of its suitability to local conditions and, so far as statute law was concerned, was increasingly obsolete. Yet this was the position which prevailed up to independence. Such attempts at improvement as were then made did not go far. In 1958 Western Nigeria took one useful step by re-enacting as local laws such English statutes as were thought to be in operation as statutes of general application and worth preserving. On re-enactment they were brought up to date by incorporating English legislation since the cut-off date. But unhappily no attempt was made to produce a code more adapted to local conditions, and I cannot think that, for example, the incorporation into the law of Western Nigeria of the English Property Legislation of 1925 was really the best way of improving the appalling confusion of land tenures. No doubt it was also a step in the right direction to abolish, as was done by some of the independence constitutions, the divergent customary criminal laws, but I cannot think that the criminal codes that then became universally applicable were really what these countries needed. They appear to me to display what has been described as "the obvious foolishness of some English legal concepts in an African society."[42] Laws, for example, which make bigamy a crime in polygamous societies or "which find a man guilty and fine him without compelling him to make restitution to the offended party or his family . . . are obviously not meant to be obeyed by sensible men."[43]

In other words, I am not very proud of the legal legacy which we have bequeathed to our colonies. But it must be admitted that this view would not be shared by most of the trained lawyers in those countries whose belief in the perfection of English law surpasses that of any Englishman, and who seem able to ignore most of the complications flowing from the duality of English and customary laws.

10. *The Economic Legacy*

On the economic legacy of colonialism, all I need say here is that on independence the colonies were in the strictest sense underdeveloped countries, and the smaller ones would obviously be hard put ever to become economically self-supporting. The vast majority of the population lived by subsistence farming, and the main economic activity was the production of raw materials (mainly agricultural) and their export to the United

[42] Ronald Wraith and Edgar Simpkins, *Corruption in Developing Societies* (London, 1963), p. 184.

[43] *Ibid.* Are we common lawyers right in supposing that the rigid separation of criminal and civil procedure represents an advance on the so-called "primitive" customary and Islamic laws which draw no such distinction?

Kingdom in exchange for manufactured goods. In some cases the control of the whole process was in expatriate hands (European or Asian); in others, the initial production of the raw material (for example West African cocoa) and the ultimate trading in the imported goods was in African hands, with expatriates controlling the intermediate processes. Secondary industry was virtually nonexistent and commerce still largely controlled by expatriate firms. All the countries embarked on independence with ambitious (if somewhat imprecise) development plans which, without a greater measure of economic collaboration, they seemed unlikely to achieve.

11. *The Emotional and Moral Legacy*

Finally, I want to refer to what I may describe as the emotional and moral legacy of colonialism. As I see it, colonialism tends to produce a kind of inferiority complex, which subsists for some time after colonialism is ended. One of its characteristics is hypersensitivity: a readiness to take offence and to resent anything that can be construed as criticism, however mild and however justified. Shortly before the American War of Independence an Englishman is reported to have said: "The trouble with the American Colonies is that they take umbrage so easily." If this had any truth when the colonial power and most of the colonial people were of the same stock, it is not surprising if the same trait is discernible in Africa, where there are differences in race and colour between colonisers and colonised. And there is no doubt that the African ex-colonies do take umbrage so easily. They are on the lookout for slights and find them where none is intended. They are particularly sensitive to criticism not only from their former overlords—the British—but from any Western country, for they tend to lump them all together as colonialists, neo-colonialists or imperialists. In this they include the United States, whom they see as dollar-imperialists striving to supplant the British as the dominant influence in Africa.[44] I do not, of course, suggest that the West should on this account refrain from criticising the African states when criticism is called for. But I do suggest that it behoves the West and the Western press to be more conscious than they appear to be of the bitter and general resentment which that criticism is likely to cause. And criticism of an African leader himself is likely to be especially resented. One can with impunity be pretty rude about Johnson, Wilson, Kosygin, Mao, or even de Gaulle, but make the same comment about Tubman, Nyerere, Banda, or Kenyatta and you will have independent Africa about your ears. For in this respect at least, Pan-African sentiment already prevails, and these are Africa's charismatic leaders who have set their people free.[45]

Another symptom of colonial neurosis is a tendency to blame anything that goes wrong on anyone but themselves. This, of course, is a trait which we all share; but African states have an ever-ready scapegoat—the former colonial power and its allies. An almost automatic response to any difficulty is to blame the expatriates. And that is a very natural and to some extent justifiable response, since until very recently the basic decisions were taken or dictated by expatriates. It is supported

44 This view is widely held in the most responsible quarters and obviously has some validity. What is irrational is the resentment to which it gives rise—both in Africa and in Britain; America is quite right to want to be a dominant influence and it is folly to resent it.

45 On the other hand, the press (or the leader) of one African state can be, and frequently is, pretty outspoken about the behaviour of another African state (or its leader).

by the promulgation of various half-believed myths, such as the myth that the British alone are responsible for the survival of tribalism, or that Peace Corps volunteers are spies for the C.I.A. Another, less common, symptom is aggressive acts designed to humiliate expatriates and to show them who is now the master.

So much for the emotional consequences. There are also moral ones. Colonialism, like enemy occupation, tends to instil a contempt for the law and for the moral standards which it expresses. The government is an alien one; to cheat it is a patriotic duty. The law is that of the colonial oppressor; it has no moral sanction and punishment for breaking it has no moral or social stigma. The political future of a nationalist in Ghana depended upon acquiring the degree of P.G. (Prison Graduate), and one leader who failed to achieve this distinction, but kept the pot boiling while his colleagues were incarcerated, had to be rewarded with an honorary P.G. degree. This belief that a conviction is an honour rather than a disgrace is not restricted to political offences.[46] Some, who afterwards attained the highest positions in newly independent African states, had been convicted of crimes of dishonesty of which their fellow Africans were the victims. No one (apart from their immediate victims) thought much the worse of them on that account.

If this moral climate automatically changed on independence all this would matter little. But it did not. It takes some time (as it did in Europe after the German occupation) for the idea to seep through that the gov-

[46] To qualify for a "P.G. hat" the offence had to be a political one. But acceptance by the community is likely irrespective of the nature of the offence. "Trained in H.M. Prisons" is still a common advertisement.

ernment is now "ours" not "theirs," and that the laws are of "our" making and ought (morally) to be obeyed. Indeed, in so far as the received law is an alien importation which does not always reflect African moral values, it will take far longer than it did in post-war Europe for people to accept it as "ours."[47]

These, then, are my eleven legacies. Most derive, as I said at the beginning, from the contradictory aims of colonialism. On the one hand, economic exploitation led to economic underdevelopment and contributed to indirect rule and to inadequate education in many areas. On the other, belief in our civilising mission led us to bequeath what we believed to be the finest fruits of British civilisation—British-style education, the Westminster, Whitehall, Sandhurst, and Scotland Yard models, the rule of law, and the common law. Both in combination produced the emotional and moral legacies.

In the lectures which follow, I shall discuss what, in the light of events since independence, seems likely to happen to these legacies and what that means in terms of the legal profession needed in these countries. Their present legal profession is, of course, itself an additional legacy of British colonialism and an important one. But that I want to reserve for my final lecture.

47 "The growth of commercial honesty and of the other qualities that are needed in the new social economy will depend both on a much fuller identification of the African with institutions felt to be genuinely his own, and on a gradual training in the moral systems which attach to the new roles." Guy Hunter, *The New Societies of Tropical Africa* (London, 1962), p. 76.

II

Post-Independence: Husbanding or Squandering the Inheritance?

In my first lecture I drew attention to certain legacies left to the African ex-dependencies on the demise of British colonial rule. In this and the succeeding lecture I want to assess what has happened to these legacies since independence, what seems likely to be the situation in these countries during the next two or three decades, and what this means in terms of the type of legal profession required in these countries.

Since Ghana, the first of these countries to attain independence, did so as recently as 1957, and others only during the past year, it may be objected that it is too early to make any intelligent prognostications. But certain trends are already very evident and these trends show a common pattern—common indeed not only to the former British territories but to all the independent African states. Many of you will find these trends regrettable and my prognostications gloomy. Let me say at once, therefore, that I do not take a gloomy view of the future. I regard it as little short of a miracle that, in all the circumstances, these states have done as well as they have. And, on the whole, I think that all of them have done remarkably well. Certainly they have made more rapid progress since independence than they did under colonialism. There have been mistakes and in some countries there have been atrocities, but there has not been general chaos or carnage. Those who say that African countries have proved incapable of ruling themselves are talking nonsense. They are ruling themselves, and their people—both black and white—are considerably happier than those in certain countries to the south. I believe that the fact that they are doing so well reflects the greatest credit on those who now rule these countries and some credit on their former colonial masters.

In assessing what has happened to the British legacies one has, as I see it, to bear in mind four fundamental differences between Britain and Africa. One is the difference between the relatively homogeneous British society and an African society divided, not only ethnically, but also socially and economically into the subsistence sector and the educated Westernised sector. The second is the demand for immediate economic progress which is used to justify or excuse an arbitrariness that would never be tolerated in England. The third is the massive governmental intervention in all African economies, whether overtly socialist or not. You may regard Britain as socialistic by your standards but far more is left to individual initiative than has proved possible in Africa. The British institutions and law which the Africans have inherited were based on that greater individualism; in Africa they are being subjected to inevitable strains. Finally, there are differences in the accepted scales of values and morality. There would be general agreement between an Englishman and an African on what is virtuous and what vicious. But there would be less agreement as to the relative importance of particular virtues and vices. Respect for truth, for age, and for position would rank differently in the unexpressed scales of values which we each try to observe. Even if we agreed about the relative importance of, say, respect for family obligations, we should differ fundamentally in our respective definitions of the family to which obligations were owed. It is subtle differences of this sort which make for difficulty when the institutions of the one come to be operated by the other.

1. *Statehood.*

The first of my legacies, statehood, has so far proved extraordinarily resistant to the stresses and strains of independence; on the whole it has resisted both the centrifugal forces of tribalism and the centripetal forces of Pan-Africanism.

The Belgian Congo has been on the verge of disintegration and so is Nigeria, but none of the other newly independent states has shown much sign of breaking-up, and most of the former British territories have displayed a remarkable degree of cohesion. A growing national pride has been manifested by all the African countries: they may be rent by internal squabbles but all the factions unite against external threats or criticisms. If the political leaders are determined to suppress tribalism instead of fomenting it, it can be damped down, if not yet totally eradicated. But experience seems to me to suggest that this demands the ruthless and rapid dismantling of federal or regional devolution on tribal lines.[1] This has been achieved in Ghana and Kenya and, to a considerable extent, in Uganda. But not in Nigeria. Nigeria attained independence without the struggle for

[1] Sir W. Arthur Lewis, of course, takes the exactly opposite view. See his *Politics in West Africa* (London, 1965).

it producing a leader who was regarded as a hero by the country as a whole. Its heroes were of particular ethnic groups and they opted for a constitution which divided the country into federated tribal states. Nothing could have been more likely to increase tribal tensions—and so it proved. Only a military coup saved Nigeria from breaking up in January 1966. Unfortunately that solved nothing, for tribalism then spread to and split the army. Even if the present crisis is surmounted, it is difficult to see how the still looser form of tribal federalism that is now contemplated can bind the country together more successfully than the old. Yet if the Congo could survive, one feels that somehow Nigeria will too.

Unfortunately, although national pride may have prevented further fragmentation it has also frustrated attempts to reduce the "balkanisation" of Africa.[2] One would have expected that adjacent states formerly under the same colonial master would tend to merge, but so far, with one possible exception, all such attempts have failed. The one exception is the recent union of Tanganyika and Zanzibar to form the United Republic of Tanzania. This, however, was something like a shotgun wedding, and it has not yet been consummated. As for the hoped-for East African Federation, that seems more remote than ever. In Africa, federalism has become a dirty word.[3] Even collaboration on the economic and technical level, has been handicapped by the determina-

2 This "balkanisation" cannot fairly be blamed on colonialism, which in most cases created far larger entities than previously existed; unfortunately they were generally not large enough. In French West Africa, moreover, there was further balkanisation on independence.

3 Many Americans would say that its failure in the Central African Federation, Kenya, Uganda, the West Indies, and Nigeria is another legacy of British rule, since the British do not understand federalism. It is a fact, however, that it has survived in a good many former British colonies, especially in those settled by people of British stock.

tion of each state to go it alone, and to go one better than the others, rather than to go in with the others for the common good.[4]

Nevertheless, growth of national feeling has, throughout independent Africa, been coupled with a strong emotional urge towards Pan-Africanism, and this urge has ultimately led to the establishment of the Organisation of African Unity. O.A.U., however, is still the loosest of alliances, directed more toward the common enemy of colonialism (and especially towards South Africa, Rhodesia, and Portugal) than toward true economic, let alone political, unity. It is, as it were, a NATO rather than an E.E.C., and still less like a United States; and at the moment it is in even greater disarray than NATO.

In the long run, however, closer collaboration seems inevitable and already certain manifestations of Pan-African feeling have had consequences on the practical level. Just as external pressures tend to unite rival tribes within each country, so do pressures external to Africa tend to unite rival African countries. Thus in international affairs the independent African states, sometimes in conjunction with the independent Asian states and sometimes on their own, have formed an alliance which wields what many regard as a disproportionate influence in the United Nations. Considering that these states had no prior experience of international diplomacy it is indeed quite remarkable how important their influence

[4] When working in 1959 to produce a new code of business corporations for Ghana I visited Nigeria to see whether there was any interest in a uniform company law for both countries. The answer I got was that Nigeria would never adopt something adopted by Ghana but would be interested only in something better. The Liberian Embassy declined to supply me with a copy of the Liberian Act in case this helped me to produce something better than the Liberian one!

has become and how skilfully they have played their hands.

Increasingly too, the African countries have shown a greater eagerness to receive military, economic, and technical aid from each other rather than from elsewhere, even from the United Nations.[5] Thus, Nigeria and Ghana have supplied judges, magistrates, and legal draftsmen to East Africa. There are also some signs of a growing recognition on the part of the new rulers that if they are to satisfy the demands of their peoples for economic development this can come only as a result of continent-wide, or at least regional, planning; in other words, they are beginning to see that this aspect of Pan-Africanism constitutes not a threat to themselves but a condition of their survival in power. Ultimately this type of collaboration may lead to closer political union, but for all the talk of Pan-Africanism and African unity, it will take a very long time.

Nevertheless, these countries have already felt the need for lawyers with a knowledge of international law and organisation and of the legal systems of African states besides their own. If closer union of any sort is ever to come, lawyers with still wider knowledge will be needed. The drafting of the requisite conventions, agreements, and constitutions is a legal task of great complexity. So is the adaptation of the existing laws of the separate states which will be inevitable if any form of political union is to be achieved. And, as a first step, the English-speaking lawyers must understand French, and the French-speaking ones, English. At present, African lawyers who are fluent in both languages are vir-

[5] Unfortunately, their military, economic, and technical resources are totally inadequate to enable them to give the help needed, for example, by the Congo, or to enable them to intervene effectively in Rhodesia.

tually non-existent. I have not forgotten a legal conference in 1961 which nearly broke up in disorder because the French-speaking Africans, taking umbrage at what they regarded, with some justification, as the inadequate translation arrangements, were about to walk out. The situation was saved only by the presence of a bilingual American lawyer who, in polished French, poured oil on the troubled waters. The hero of that occasion, Harvard's Professor Arthur Sutherland, will not have forgotten it either. Talk of Pan-Africanism makes little sense unless the Africans of one state can understand the Africans of another. And such understanding is particularly vital among their lawyers.

2. *Membership of the Commonwealth*

My second legacy, membership of the Commonwealth, is one which, I suggested, can have meant very little to the African states up to the time when they achieved independence. Nevertheless, it is one to which all have clung. They have clung to it not from any sentimental attachment, nor even, I think, because it has afforded them any substantial economic advantages. Mainly it is because it has given them another international organisation in which they can make their influence felt. The Commonwealth is still important on the international scene, and they are an increasingly important influence within the Commonwealth. At Commonwealth Prime Ministers' Conferences they, in combination, constitute the largest bloc, and, with the Asian members, who are likely to feel as they do on most issues, an overwhelming majority. Their power, which they showed when they drove South Africa out, is the greater because their attachment to the Commonwealth *is* unemotional so that the shock to them, if the exercise of their power broke up the Commonwealth, would be far less than in the Dominions whose citizens are mainly of British stock. In every case it may safely be assumed that they would put African unity before the Commonwealth, as ex-President Nkrumah showed when he sought a union with the non-Commonwealth states of Guinea and Mali. But as yet they have not had to make that choice: the Rhodesian crisis may face them with it, but so far none has left the Commonwealth on that account (even President Kaunda would prefer that Britain should be expelled, rather than that Zambia should walk out). And, as that crisis has shown, the Commonwealth in many ways means more to them than to Britain and the older Dominions. The latter tend to think of it as a family gathering where respectful salutations are paid to the Mother Country. To the new Afro-Asian members it is a genuine international organisation where scant respect need be paid to Mother. This is not always to the liking of the older generation but my guess is that the Commonwealth will survive, although its nature will be transformed under Afro-Asian influence. Already it is very different from what it was at the time of the Balfour Declaration, the Statute of Westminster, or even the withdrawal of South Africa.

3. *The Legacy of Indirect Rule*

I called my third legacy the legacy of indirect rule. As I pointed out, the policy of indirect rule was reversed after the Second World War, and all that remained at independence were certain social and educational relics. Since independence, determined efforts have been made to eradicate these, but not always, as it seems to me, in a way which is wholly desirable.

In British West Africa (much less so in East Africa)

any overt manifestations of a colour bar or white superiority had disappeared before independence and so, indeed, had most of the feelings which it engenders. An English girl once remarked to me at a Highlife session in Accra: "Here an African can ask an English girl to dance; she can say no, and it won't occur to either that her refusal is because he is black and she is white." On the other hand in both West and East Africa the expatriate still continued to enjoy certain privileges which were denied to all but a very small minority of Africans. Normally he lived in plusher accommodation in one of the exclusive residential areas. He would have a car and often a driver. His leave entitlement would be such as to enable him to proceed home between short tours. And it would be unthinkable that he should undertake any sort of menial task.[6] To enable him to enjoy these advantages his basic pay would be supplemented by numerous allowances.

The eradication of these social distinctions between black and white has not come about by denying the whites these advantages, but by upgrading an African elite so that its members enjoy them too. As Africans have increasingly come to hold jobs which formerly would have been held by expatriates they have assumed not only the salaries but also the social superiority, the amenities, the allowances and the fringe benefits which expatriate holders of these jobs formerly enjoyed. In West Africa this has already gone to ludicrous lengths and contributed to social and industrial unrest.[7] Minis-

6 This linking of status with superiority to manual labour has had lamentable consequences. There is, of course, a small minority which fights against it and insists on doing its own chores.

7 Cf. the Nigerian General Strike of June 1964, and the *Report of the Morgan Commission on the Review of Wages, Salaries, and Conditions of Service* (Lagos: Federal Ministry of Information, 1964).

ters and government employees move out of their own houses, let them at high rentals, often payable years in advance, and go into lavish government quarters for which they pay rents representing only a tithe of their true annual value. They are given loans to enable them to buy cars and then paid "motor-car basic allowances" to enable them to run the cars and repay the loans.[8] Employees who, in England or America, would be content with two or three weeks' holiday each year get two months or more, despite the acute shortage of trained administrators. Ministers emphasise their importance by living in mansions and by riding everywhere in cars which outdo in size and magnificence those of their former colonial masters. Cars, indeed, are the great status symbols (you will understand that) and no one earning more than about $2,000 per annum is prepared to do without one. And all this in countries where the average income per head of population is in most cases under £25 (about $75) per annum.

In fairness it should be said that the new governments are faced with a difficult problem. It may be that initially it is necessary for them to rule with the regal magnificence of the colonial governors, if only to prove to their people that they are now the masters in their own home. And while they still need expatriate help they can attract it only by continuing to offer to expatriates colonial amenities and allowances which, in general, are not unreasonable in their case. If they deny them to Africans in comparable positions, then they continue the discrimination between Africans and expatriates which all are anxious to avoid. It is true that

8 The total expended by the Nigerian governments in basic car allowances alone was £4,389,895 in 1960-63; see the *Report of the Morgan Commission*, p. 47.

most expatriates could live a lot more cheaply than they do; if British and American experts continue to demand a standard of living as high (or higher) than that to which they have been accustomed, it will be natural if the African countries say: "We don't want you. We'd rather get help from countries like Israel and China whose experts are more prepared to live on our own level." Nevertheless some discrimination is justified and essential simply because an expatriate cannot live as cheaply as a native of the place and because, as a temporary visitor, he must be found accommodation and given the leave entitlement that will enable him to visit his home and family. In any case, conspicuous expenditure and ostentatious living by the new elites already go far beyond what is necessary to avoid discrimination between black and white and seem designed, rather, to emphasise and widen the social rift between the elite and the man in the street. Members of an alien, autocratic colonial government may have thought it necessary to preserve this rift; there can be no justification for the continuation of a still wider one between democratic African governments and the mass of the people. The real tragedy is that all this is leading to a corrosive cynicism which is corrupting the earlier idealism that characterised the nationalist movements and constituted the most encouraging hope for the future.

I often said that the great day for Nigeria would be when one of the ministers went to his office on a bicycle rather than in a chauffeur-driven limousine. But they did not heed that advice and they paid the penalty. On the other hand it must be admitted that most members of the public did not appear to think much the worse of them because they feathered their nests and displayed their plumage. It was only the intellectuals (who, as in most underdeveloped countries, included the military officers and some trade unionists) who bitterly resented it. The attitude of the general public was rather: good luck to them—so long as we share some of the spoils. In both Nigeria and Ghana the military revolts had public support partly because the spoils had not been shared but monopolised by the elite.

The military regimes in West Africa have gone to great lengths to denounce the ostentation of their predecessors. This, unfortunately, is not the same thing as eradicating it for the future. But they have declared their intention to do that too and it is to be hoped that they will succeed and that other countries will learn the lesson. At present, however, this is the environment in which the legal profession has to operate; and lawyers are, par excellence, members of the elite. In West Africa, where there was a sizeable legal profession before independence, lawyers were among the earliest and perhaps the most influential members of that elite. Law is still the prestige profession and lawyers feel that they have to maintain themselves according to the elite's social standards. Their offices may be scruffy—that is in the accepted tradition of the Inns of Court—but a Mercedes is a must. Yet unless they have salaried posts, they will be hard put to it to pay for the Mercedes. There are few salaried legal posts outside the government service—hence the tendency to seek government jobs rather than private practice. If they remain in private practice they will be subject to great temptations to pay for the needed status symbols out of their clients' money or, at least, to maximise their charges by encouraging their clients to indulge in prolonged and expensive litigation. If they join the public service they will be subject to temptations of a different sort, to which I will refer later.

It is my impression that West Africa ("British" and "French") has been far worse in these respects than East Africa where, for example, President Nyerere's regime in Tanganyika appears positively austere in comparison.[9] And it may be that the recent military coups will usher in a new era of austerity in West Africa too. It is, as yet, too early to say.

4. *The Educational System*

The fourth legacy was the educational system, which has been greatly developed, but not wholly transformed. The missionary element, for example, remains strongly entrenched in the management (as opposed to the financing and the educational policy) of the schools. And in East Africa the "integration" of the three separate school systems—African, Asian, and European—is still in its infancy.

One of the most heartening features of independent Africa is the passion for education. Governments will spend a quarter or more of their revenues on it; parents, uncles (and even more remote members of the extended African family) will cheerfully bear the greatest hardships in order to educate their young; children themselves will display a wholehearted dedication to their studies such as is rarely seen in Europe or America. The tragedy is that the quality of the education is still, all too often, unworthy of the amount spent on it or of the passionate dedication.

At the apex of the educational pyramid there has been a sensational increase in the number of universi-

[9] There have been cuts in ministerial salaries and real efforts have been made to identify the political elite with the ordinary people. Recently ministers have had their Mercedes withdrawn and been told to buy their own cars.

ties. In place of the four university colleges in West and East Africa prior to independence, there are now thirteen universities or university colleges; five in Nigeria (three regional and two federal), three in Ghana, two in Sierra Leone, and one each in Kenya, Uganda, and Tanganyika. In independent southern Africa there are three more.[10]

The traditional view that the humanities, and especially the classics, are a better mental training than science or technology still lingers on, but the more recent foundations are striving to counteract it. The local study of medicine and engineering is at last receiving its deserved place and law is perhaps receiving too much emphasis—it is taught at four of the five Nigerian universities—an example of the wasteful duplication of effort which the National Universities Commission is seeking to correct. And despite the efforts of that commission and of the Nigerian governments, nearly 60 per cent of university students are reading the humanities and social sciences whereas at least that proportion should instead be studying the natural sciences or technology.

Efforts are being made to lengthen the academic year and to ensure that the universities' plant is used for more than seven months in the year. Encouraged by freedom from London's apron-strings, attempts are being made to Africanise the syllabuses.[11] British and American schemes for "topping-up" the salaries of expatriate teachers have at last made it possible for the African universities to detach themselves from British

10 Four, if one includes Rhodesia. The three are in Zambia, Malawi, and Lesotho (formerly Basutoland).

11 This is not intended to imply that the former failure to Africanise was the fault of London University; it was in fact much more the fault of the local teachers.

salary scales and to introduce for the growing numbers of African teachers something more in key with the general level of African incomes. As yet, however, most universities have not made up their minds whether or not there should be different arrangements regarding conditions of service between Africans and expatriates. Once again the difficulty is to reconcile the desire for non-discrimination and the continuing need to attract teachers from abroad.

Another problem is to maintain academic freedom and to prevent undue interference from governments which tend to think that he who pays the piper calls the tune, and that a university is just another public corporation to be used for purposes of political patronage and influence. It was an Asian, not an African prime minister who told the students of the University of Lagos that in the newly independent states "the intellectual elite must march in step with the political elite, otherwise momentum will be lost."[12] But this view would appeal to many African leaders, and few of these leaders would be prepared to recognize that one of the supporting roles of the academic elite is to offer objective criticism of the political elite, especially where other sources of criticism, such as the press or a parliamentary opposition, have been silenced.

Facilities for higher technical training have not expanded at the same pace, and a number of former technical institutes, such as the various branches of the Nigerian College of Arts and Sciences, the Kumasi College of Technology, and the Royal Technical College, Nairobi, have been converted into universities. The passion, unfortunately, is still for education fitting for white-collar employment, not for that which involves dirtying one's

12 Mr. Lee Kuan Yew, Prime Minister of Singapore.

hands.[13] Hence, education has not led to the much needed improvement in agriculture; the educated leave the land and seek more prestigious employment in the towns.

Primary and secondary education have increased but, again, hardly in proportion to the facilities for university education, especially at the secondary level; in prestige, one new university equals two hundred new schools. More serious is the qualitative lag, especially in West Africa.[14] On the whole, teaching standards are low and teaching methods unimaginative, with too much emphasis on learning by rote and too little on understanding and original thought. There are far too few properly trained or really dedicated teachers, and the universities tend to siphon off teachers instead of being a source of them. It is still all too common to leave school without achieving the educational standards needed for university entrance and to take a teaching post, not as a long-term career, but because this offers the best opportunity for studying for the examinations needed to qualify for entry to a university. Once these examinations have been passed university entrance is sought and school-teaching left for all time.[15] When I

13 "The implication and the influences of the inherited system of education in schools have led potentially excellent cabinet-makers into becoming no-account lawyers, and potentially first-class bread-makers or dressmakers into becoming fourth-class teachers or inefficient secretary-typists." O. Ikejiani, *Nigerian Education* (Lagos, 1964), p. 87.

14 "African secondary schools in East Africa with 100 per cent trained teachers, with a high percentage of graduates, are still far ahead of most West African countries—because the teachers are still largely expatriates." Guy Hunter, *Education for a Developing Region* (London, 1963), p. 9.

15 Yet it has been stated that a minimum of one-third of all university graduates should enter the teaching profession; see Frederick Harbison, "The African University and Human Resources Development"; a paper delivered at the Conference on The African University and National Educational Development, Teachers' College, Columbia University, September 8-18, 1964.

interviewed the first intake of law students at the University of Lagos I found that one was the principal of a secondary school. I said to him: "But you have an important post. Why do you want to throw it up to read for a law degree?" He answered: "Because I want to become a member of a profession." "But teaching is a profession," I said. "Oh, no," he replied, "not in Nigeria." While that attitude persists it is difficult to see how school standards will improve. Until they do there is a grave risk that when the new universities are in full operation there will, in certain subjects, be too many university places chasing too few qualified students.

An increasing proportion of young people are learning fluent English. But increasingly what is taught is an African English which diverges from British English. As I said in my first lecture, this would not matter if it were a precise and clear English. All too often, however, it is the sort which encourages verbosity, a passion for long, impressive-sounding words, and general sloppiness of thought.[16]

Efforts are at last being made to make school-leaving and university entrance examinations, and therefore school curricula, more relevant to African conditions. But as yet, these have not borne much fruit; school-leavers are likely still to know English, but not African, history; Latin, but not French; and to have "done" Jane Austen but never read any of the African novelists.

Unfortunately, as I think, the tendency in both West

16 A recent report goes even further. "It has often been remarked that education in West Africa presents a paradox; the schooling is almost wholly verbal, yet the child at the end of it is virtually inarticulate and almost illiterate." D. W. Grieve, *Report of an Inquiry into English Language Examining* (Lagos, 1964), p. 10. The implementation of Mr. Grieve's excellent report affords a real hope of improvement.

and East Africa is to follow the English concept of the secondary school "sixth form" where study is specialised and on a level equivalent to that of the first two years at an American liberal arts college. If such studies had been concentrated in colleges attached to the universities more economic use could have been made of the small number of top-level teachers and of laboratory and library facilities. Moreover, the higher status flowing from the attachment to the universities might have encouraged more good people to take up teaching as a career. But it is probably too late now to advocate that; there are already too many sixth forms and school authorities place too much value on the prestige which they are thought to confer on their schools.[17] Moreover, most African educationalists, who have obtained an English-style education, are suspicious of any American educational ideas. The undoubted success of Peace Corps teachers may be breaking down this prejudice to some extent, though it is unfortunate that corps volunteers have too often been employed in sixth form work, for which their training has not equipped them.

The belief that any educational qualification will open the door to white-collar employment is still clung to in pathetic disregard of the facts. In conditions of growing urban unemployment and chronic under-employment it is no longer certain that even the output

[17] This is a very recent development: "The number of African VIth Forms in the whole of Nyasaland, Northern and Southern Rhodesia and the three East African territories put together did not reach ten in 1960." Guy Hunter, *The New Societies of Tropical Africa* (London, 1962), p. 245. In 1960 there were only twenty-two (mostly excessively small) in the whole of Nigeria: *Investment in Education,* the Report of the [Ashby] Committee on Post-School Certificate and Higher Education in Nigeria (Lagos, 1960), pp. 12, 75. In Zambia, and in the former High Commission Territories of Basutoland, Bechuanaland, and Swaziland where there are still no sixth forms, the policy is that the equivalent of sixth form work shall be undertaken at the universities.

of the new universities can be absorbed into the sort of jobs for which the graduates' training primarily equips them. Planning here is handicapped by the absence of detailed and accurate manpower projections.

Despite the increase in local facilities there is still an eagerness for overseas education. Parents who can afford it—and some can—still tend to send their children to schools and universities in the United Kingdom, or to the Inns of Court. But more distant relatives and clan and tribal organisations are increasingly reluctant to provide finance for this purpose and governments, by their scholarship policies, actively discourage it.[18] The social cachet attached in West Africa to the "been-to" is waning though it has not disappeared. There is now a somewhat ambivalent attitude towards the highly Anglicised African, and in political life too-Oxford an accent and too-Savile Row a suit may be a positive handicap; they do not fit snugly on the "African personality."

These then are some of the features of the present educational background; these are the schools and universities in which the African lawyer of the future will receive his education and basic legal training. I am quite sure that the education and training can be and will be better for him than what he received in the past. But, as I hope I have illustrated, there are difficulties still to be overcome. Africanisation of the educational system may have proceeded further than in francophonic Africa, but anglophonic Africa is still a long way from completing the adaptation of the British model so that it meets specifically African needs—needs which de-

18 The discouragement is especially strong and effective in East Africa; students are not allowed to accept overseas scholarships for undergraduate study overseas if they have satisfied the entrance requirements of the University of East Africa and wish to study subjects available there.

mand broad secondary education because so many pupils come from illiterate homes; emphasis on technological skills needed for rapid agricultural and industrial development; and study of the humanities and social and natural sciences in relation to the culture and conditions of Africa.

5. *The Westminster Model*

From the very beginning, the Westminster model of representative parliamentary government functioned very differently in Africa and after a few years it has everywhere been transformed almost out of recognition. Some governments still remain "representative" and "parliamentary" in the sense that the population, by the exercise of their votes, have an opportunity of changing the government, and in the sense that there is a legislature with members elected by the public. But in all the countries with which I am primarily concerned the main distinguishing features of the Westminster model are rapidly disappearing or have already disappeared—in practice and sometimes in law. This transformation, to my mind, is not directly due to a lack of literacy and education on the part of the electorate—the traditional reason for reluctance to grant self-government. In my observation, Africans, literate or illiterate, exercise their franchise (when allowed to do so) just as rationally as we in the West. This, of course, is not saying much. It is sheer humbug to pretend that the British electorate exercises a high degree of ratiocination when it votes. Most of us vote Labour because we are Labour, or Conservative because we are Conservative; just as most of you vote Democrat because you are Democrats, or Republican because you are Republican. (Would Senator Goldwater have collected twenty-six million votes otherwise?) On the other hand, illiteracy may well have contributed to the destruction of an organised Opposition, since governments are understandably reluctant to explain their policies fully to a population incapable of grasping the complications and equally reluctant to allow others to attack those policies in necessarily oversimplified terms.[19]

In describing the transformation that has occurred I ignore what I regard as relatively unimportant changes of form, such as the trend towards unicameral rather than bicameral legislatures, and concentrate on what seem to me to be fundamental changes. The first of these is in the relationship between the legislature and the executive. Ghana, Nigeria, Kenya, and Tanzania have become republics, and so, further south, have Zambia and Malawi. Sierra Leone intends to. Uganda (though perhaps not technically a republic) has its own head of state. Where, as in Nigeria and at first in Uganda, this amounted to no more than substituting an African non-executive president for the Queen acting through an African governor-general, the change was unimportant except in terms of local pride and sentiment. But in Ghana, Kenya, Tanzania, and now Uganda, as in Zambia and Malawi, it meant much more, for the president became the chief executive, taking the former place of the Queen, the governor general, and the prime minister—a move, if you like, from the Westminster toward the Washington model.

In my view this is the inevitable pattern of future development. A figurehead on the ship of state makes

19 See S. A. de Smith, *The New Commonwealth and Its Constitutions* (London, 1964), pp. 237-38. It also enables politicians to get away with bigger and more blatant lies than would be possible with a more educated public.

little sense unless, as with Her Britannic Majesty, its nakedness is draped with an emotional aura.[20] Even if that is so, a traditional ruler will find it difficult to behave like an impotent constitutional monarch—as the Kabaka found in Uganda.[21] A former nationalist leader will find it equally difficult, as President Azikiwe showed during the 1964-65 Nigerian crisis. Yet Uganda and Nigeria appeared to be countries in which there was especial justification for a non-executive president—one part of the country might thereby be reconciled to the vesting of true power in another by balancing the title of greatest honour against the position of greatest power. In neither did it work.

A change to an executive president would also be relatively unimportant if the president, in the exercise of his executive powers, were responsible to parliament to the same extent as is the prime minister under the Westminster Model. But this was not the case. In Kenya and Uganda a considerable measure of responsibility to parliament has still been retained, but very little in Tanzania and still less in Ghana during the Nkrumah regime. Nor were the same elaborate checks and balances that control the executive freedom of, say, the American president inserted to replace the diminished control of parliament.

This *de jure* alteration in the balance of power between legislature and executive in many of these countries has, *de facto*, been matched to a greater or lesser

20 In a multi-party state a president aloof from party politics may occasionally have a useful role to perform (e.g., in choosing a prime minister or refusing a dissolution of parliament to a defeated prime minister); this, no doubt, accounts for the retention of a non-executive president in the draft republican constitution of Sierra Leone. In a one-party state he lacks even this justification.

21 And the Paramount Chief in Basutoland (Lesotho).

extent everywhere else. The reason for this is that nowhere does parliament and the party system function at all as it does in Britain. The parliament at Westminster sits for about six months in the year. Bills go through an elaborate process of a formal first reading; a second reading, during which the policy of the bill as a whole is debated; committee stage, during which the details are scrutinised either by the whole house or by a smaller standing committee; report stage, when the bill, as amended in committee, is reconsidered; and, finally, the third reading. This process takes place in each house, and there is a substantial interval between each stage, which normally takes several days and sometimes weeks. Ample opportunity is also provided for questioning and criticising government action—at question time, on motions for the adjournment, on private members' motions and so on.

On paper, until the recent coups suspending the legislatures in Ghana, Nigeria, and Sierra Leone, the position was virtually identical in the states of former British Africa. In practice it was totally different; first, because their parliaments did not, in fact, operate like that, and secondly, because of the atrophy of the Opposition. Let me illustrate the first point by the practice of the former federal parliament of Nigeria—I choose this because it was widely believed until this year that Nigeria was the one country in which the Westminster model still functioned more or less unchanged—and because Professor John Mackintosh has done my work for me.[22]

Parliament met for only three short sittings each year,

22 See J. P. Mackintosh's "The Nigerian Federal Parliament" [1963] *Public Law*, p. 333—to which I must acknowledge my indebtedness. For an expanded version, see his *Nigerian Government and Politics* (London, 1966), chap. iii.

for a total of about forty days in the case of the House of Representatives and twenty days in the case of the Senate.[23] Bills were usually taken through all stages in one day and often four or five bills were taken in a day. Every stage except the second reading was a formality. The committee stage—all-important in England for detailed scrutiny—was always taken in committee of the whole house and disposed of in a few minutes; it performed no useful purpose except to enable the government to correct any mistakes discovered at the last minute. So far, therefore, as the process of legislation was concerned parliament merely rubber-stamped government legislation. Very occasionally it refused to affix its stamp; but it was not allowed to do this unless the Council of Ministers was seriously divided on the policy of the bill.[24]

As for opportunities to criticise government action and policy, these were few and little used. The leader of the house exercised rigid control of business, and private members' motions embarrassing to the government came up infrequently. There were no days (as there are at Westminster) in which the Opposition could choose the business and put down motions of censure.[25] Ten days' notice of questions was necessary and, with such short sittings, this was often impossible. Ministers gen-

23 For this, members received salaries and allowances which, by African standards, would have been quite generous for a full-time job. And they found ample opportunities for making more on the side. To get elected, however, was a costly process.

24 One of the very few occasions on which the government experienced serious difficulty with parliament was in 1962 in connection with the Legal Education Bill (see Chapter 3, *infra*). These difficulties were not from the Opposition as such, but from members and senators whose personal interests were affected, i.e., lawyers and those related to students at the Inns of Court.

25 One of Chief Awolowo's complaints was that his attempts to move motions of censure were always rendered abortive.

erally refused to answer supplementary questions and avoided issues raised on motions for the adjournment by not being present. At one time the Public Accounts Committee had an Opposition chairman and, basing itself on reports by the Director of Federal Audit, was highly critical; the Opposition chairman was removed and the committee's voice hushed. Afterwards, criticisms by the Director of Audit, if ventilated in parliament, were met by criticisms of the Director.

Professor Mackintosh concluded that: "In general the control exercised by the House . . . over the executive is negligible."[26] This somewhat discouraging description of the role of parliament could have been matched in any of the other countries[27] and outmatched in Ghana.

Turning to the second reason, the atrophy of the Opposition, the trend throughout Africa is unmistakable. It is most noticeable in the case of the former French territories but is certainly not limited to them. Ghana became a one party state *de facto* and *de jure*. She is now ruled by a military junta which has dissolved that one party. The promised new constitution is hardly likely to restore the Westminster model—though it may pretend to. Ever since independence, Tanganyika has been one party in fact and has recently become so in law. Kenya, too, embarked on republicanism under one-

26 [1963] *Public Law*, p. 352.

27 "The [Tanganyika] Constituent Assembly [parliament under another name] passed the Bill for the Constitution and fourteen other Bills through all their stages in a sitting lasting little more than two hours; a few minor amendments to the Bills were moved by Ministers and approved without discussion; none of the Bills was opposed or debated." de Smith, *New Commonwealth*, p. 249. Also see J. P. W. B. McAuslan, "The Republican Constitution of Tanganyika," in (1964) 13 *International and Comparative Law Quarterly*, 502. In 1963 the Tanganyika single-chamber parliament sat for a total of thirty-one days, during which seventy-three bills were passed (*ibid.*, p. 540).

party rule, and a recent attempt by a dissident faction to re-establish an Opposition has met with little success.[28] The other former British territories are clearly set on a similar path. When, in March 1967, the Opposition in Sierra Leone was within an ace of achieving power by constitutional means, the military intervened.

From this trend there was, once again, no reason to exclude Nigeria. Prior to the military coup, as a result of each further election and of "jumping on the bandwagon" between elections, one party assumed overwhelming control in each region, and a combination of those parties assumed control at the federal level.[29] Until 1962 there was an Opposition at the centre consisting of the Action Group, the party then in power in the West. But since the A.G. disintegrated there was none there either. At the last federal elections the surviving parties fought bitterly—and unfairly—but after the fight an uneasy "coalition," "broadly based" or "national" Government emerged.[30] That was so weak and divided that it could not suppress the popular unrest after the grossly rigged election in Western Nigeria in October 1965, and after the assassination of the prime minister—the one minister who still retained any real influence or popular respect—could agree on only one course—to abdicate in favour of the army. The military have now dissolved all the parties.

28 In part this was due to a constitutional amendment which forced any M.P. who crossed the floor to seek re-election. In different circumstances, for example in Nigeria, the existence of such a rule might have arrested the atrophy of the Opposition.

29 For a fuller analysis, see J. P. Mackintosh, "Electoral Trends and the Tendency to a One Party System in Nigeria," in (1962) 1 *Journal of Commonwealth Political Studies,* 194; and cf. his articles in (1963) 11 *Political Studies,* 126 and [1963] *Public Law,* p. 333, and his *Nigerian Government and Politics,* chap. xii.

30 For a full account, see Mackintosh, *Nigerian Government and Politics,* chap. xiii.

The reasons for this general decay of the party system are many: the reluctance of politicians to play what seems to them to be the purely negative role of an Opposition in the building-up of a new state; their eagerness to share in the spoils of office and to see that their supporters share in new developments; the reluctance of those in power to countenance organised opposition; the difficulty of evolving policy differences to distinguish one party from another where there is little to disagree about except who should wield power; and recognition of the fact that opposing parties distinguished on tribal lines are likely to aggravate tensions. But the basic reason, as I see it, is that the whole conception of a standing Loyal Opposition is totally alien to African experience. I do not mean by this that indigenous African institutions do not countenance opposition and criticism. They do. Nor do I mean that they are necessarily autocratic in the sense that a traditional ruler does not have to consult with his people and retain their confidence. He generally does. What I mean is that they do not recognise a particular body of people whose regular role is to oppose. Nor is this surprising. It is, after all, a very strange notion. It may have some merit in the running of a modern state but it would not occur to anyone to operate anything else on these lines. We would not think of running a business corporation by dividing the stockholders or the directors into a standing government and opposition.[31]

The conception that Opposition can and should be "loyal" is equally strange because it is contrary to expe-

31 We may, as under the American system of cumulative voting for directors, seek to ensure that all major interests are represented on the board, but we hope that the board will combine to govern the company and not split into two rigid opposing groups.

rience in these countries prior to independence. As Frank Sutton has pointed out in a perceptive article, a colonial regime is necessarily authoritarian and cannot allow an organised Opposition to function as it would in a parliamentary democracy.[32] What in England or the United States would be treated as legitimate criticism of an existing government by a shadow government which will replace it, is necessarily treated as disloyal because it will lead to disobedience of the government. When criticism is suppressed, plots against the colonial government are likely to be resorted to and to be more rigorously suppressed. On the grant of internal self-government before independence there may, for a short time (the time was very short in Africa), be an indigenous government and opposition, but they are likely to spend much of their time combining in "disloyal" opposition to the retention of the reserved powers of the colonial regime. When independence is granted, the former combined opposition to the colonial regime is expected to fall apart, the majority constituting the government and the minority the Loyal Opposition. But independent governments headed by charismatic leaders who have led their countries to freedom do not find it any easier than a colonial regime to stomach organised opposition; their task may be still more difficult since the withdrawal of the colonial power may lead to a resurgence of tribalism. And the Opposition does not find it easy to tread the narrow path between legitimate criticism and disaffection. Its attempts to perform its prescribed role are likely to antagonise both the government and the public. The

32 Francis X. Sutton, "Authority and Authoritarianism in the New Africa," in Robert O. Tilman and Taylor Cole (eds.), *The Nigerian Political Scene* (Durham, N.C., 1962), p. 271.

government resorts to repression, as the colonial government did, the frustrated Opposition resorts to plots, as the nationalist movements did, and the government to sterner repression. The end is the end of an Opposition. The only thing surprising about all this is that anyone is surprised by it. But the British are—surprised and distressed. We still expect our former colonies to be like us.

All this does not mean that opposition, with a small "o," has been or is being destroyed. In most of these countries there is still plenty of it. But it does not manifest itself through an organised Opposition in parliament. In Ghana, it took place mainly within the party and was not allowed to hit the headlines until it erupted in gunfire; in Nigeria it took the form of public statements by one minister criticising the policy of another or even of a government whip seeking to move a motion of no confidence in a minister. All this was much more in accordance with traditional African methods. But it was not in accordance with the Westminster model.[33] Ultimately in both countries it took the form of a military take-over in response to popular unrest, closely analogous to the de-stooling of a chief who had lost his people's confidence.

Still less does all this mean that these countries are hell-bent towards communist dictatorship. Of that I can see very little evidence. The disturbing feature is that hitherto one-party government has tended to lead eventually to communist dictatorship and that communism is one of the few ideologies that has worked out

[33] Public disagreement between ministers on matters of government policy is, of course, totally inconsistent with the doctrine of collective responsibility which is embodied in the constitutions, often in a more extreme form than under the Westminster practice; see, for example, the Nigerian Federal Constitution, s. 90.

a system for operating one-party rule. Personally, I would not necessarily be unduly distressed if these countries did eventually embrace communism in its modern guise of state capitalism; if they are to solve their problems some form of state control and planning is clearly essential and their colonial masters gave them a bit more experience of that than of parliamentary democracy. I should be alarmed only if this led them to join the Eastern bloc in opposition to the West. This seems to me to be most unlikely. Their determination to remain non-aligned is sincere and deep-rooted, and their suspicion of Russia and China is as great as or greater than their suspicion of the West—the devil they know. They are prepared to accept whatever aid the East offers and to play the East off against the West and vice versa; they have played this game with considerable finesse. Since the West has been entrenched for decades and the Eastern bloc has been excluded, non-alignment demands some concessions to the East.[34] But they are not prepared to exchange domination by Western imperialists for domination by Eastern imperialists, and whenever Russia or China has appeared to be attempting to put a finger too deeply into their domestic pie, they (as in Guinea and Malawi) or their neighbours (as in Zanzibar) have reacted sharply. In Ghana the influence of Russia or China was never very great but the first act of the new military regime was to expel all their advisers and technicians. Whatever white rulers may say, liberation movements in Africa were not and are not controlled by Russia or China; neither are the new independent states.

[34] Cf. President Nyerere's powerful reply to expressions of Western alarm when he accepted eleven Chinese (seven instructors and four interpreters) to retrain his army. *The Times* (London), September 1, 1964.

Nevertheless, I would certainly prefer—so would you and so would most African politicians—that the movement toward a planned economy—however free from Eastern domination—stopped short of communism, dictatorship (military or civilian), or even one-party rule of the customary type. The great need is to evolve some new political institutions in place of the Westminster model, which has not worked in Africa, but also to find institutions which will preserve the advantages which that model has over a communist, military, or other dictatorship. The new model, however, must openly recognise that for the foreseeable future the executive will govern without effective check from the legislature, that the latter will merely say yea or nay to legislation proposed by the executive, and that opportunities for public criticism must be found otherwise than through an organised Opposition.[35]

The greatest weakness of the one-party or no-party system is its almost inevitable tendency to suppress public criticism of governmental action. Criticism is desirable not merely on libertarian grounds but also in the interests of efficiency. All governments make mistakes sometimes, and inexperienced governments faced with unprecedented problems make more (and bigger ones) than most. The best way of seeing that mistaken policies are reconsidered is to ensure that they are ventilated. Intra-party revolts may sometimes lead to change—as

[35] Sir W. Arthur Lewis considers that the solution in plural societies such as those of West Africa is federalism plus a coalition government of all the main parties at the centre (*Politics in West Africa*). Unfortunately Nigerian experience suggests that the centre coalition is unlikely to work as a united team but rather as a disparate group of individuals, each pursuing his own policy, subject to an occasional curb from his party or from the cabinet. Lewis concedes (see pp. 84-85) that his solution will not work without a fundamental change in the politicians' approach to politics.

Mr. Khrushchev found—but not always. Stalin's mistaken policies which, we are now told, inflicted unnecessary sufferings on the Russian people, were not exposed or corrected until he died. The new African model must somehow correct this weakness. Under a one-party or no-party state this can only be done if there is a formal organisation which ensures adequate democratic discussion of policy.

The other great weakness of one-party rule, the difficulty of providing for peaceful and constitutional changes of government, is of course one of its great attractions to an existing government. Retention of the Westminster model does not necessarily make changes any easier; as Nigerian experience showed, if a government is determined to cling to power it will do so until ousted by force. But under a one-party or no-party system it may be able to retain power without resort to improper practices and those who wish to oust it may themselves have to act illegally—as in Ghana. What at present seems to be happening throughout Africa is that the military are assuming the role of government-makers and breakers, which inevitably means that, for a time at least, the military has to govern. In Nigeria and Ghana (but less clearly in Sierra Leone) the army acted in response to public opinion and expressed an apparently sincere desire to hand over to civilian rule as soon as possible. But that may not be very soon. A government of technocrats—military and civil—may prove more difficult to change than the government it ousted unless, as it almost has in Nigeria, it commits suicide.

In any case, a system of dictatorship curbed by military coups is obviously undesirable. It smacks too much of the description of czarist Russia—despotism tempered by assassination. It makes it impossible for any ruler to trust his army and it makes Pan-African harmony still more difficult. Even a ruler who owes his own position to a military coup is likely to boggle at recognising a new regime installed in this way; he may be the next to be thus toppled.[36] Continued military coups could destroy O.A.U.; the Ghanaian coup very nearly did so.

One's confidence that the African states would evolve a satisfactory African model to replace the Westminster model has been sapped by a fear that the initial idealism of the African nationalist movements was being eroded by self-seeking. But recent events, however traumatic, are not wholly discouraging. Nigeria, Ghana, and Sierra Leone have now shown that there is a limit to what they are prepared to stomach even from the leaders who have freed them from the yoke of colonialism. This lesson is unlikely to be lost on others. There is now an opportunity to create new constitutions which really will be adapted to African conditions. As yet, as it seems to me, the former British territory which has made the most serious efforts in the right direction is Tanganyika. The new interim constitution, greatly as it diverges from the Westminster (or the Washington) model, is a serious attempt to design a one-party state in which there is adequate opportunity both for overt criticism of the party and for constitutional changes of government by the electorate. It will be interesting to see to what extent its experiment is followed by the constitution-makers in West Africa. But much experimentation remains to be done before the perfect model is found, and in that experimentation lawyers will have a prominent role to play.

[36] Note Nasser's reaction to the ousting of Nkrumah. The Nigerian governments obligingly avoided posing this dilemma by "voluntarily" handing over their powers, thus giving a semblance of legal and constitutional authority to the military regime.

6. *The Whitehall Model*

The Whitehall model for the public service has, as yet, proved somewhat more viable in African soil that the Westminster model. Even where military coups have occurred and the constitutions been suspended, the civil service has been left intact and virtually unpurged, and has continued to function with a measure of efficiency. But since independence there have been radical transformations in its size and racial composition. The most startling change is in size. The small administrative organisations which sufficed somehow until independence have now been enormously inflated.[37] The old Secretariat in Lagos which at one time housed the whole central administration for a united Nigeria became barely adequate for one ministry of the federal administration alone. This increase could hardly have been achieved without some lowering of standards; nor has it. Trained talent has been spread far too thin. Partly for this reason it has not proved possible to introduce adequate devolution of responsibility; experience in most of these countries soon teaches that if you want an answer or action it is always advisable to approach the minister or the permanent secretary and often quite useless to start on a lower level. Good people at the top have far too much to do. Good new recruits at the bottom are under-employed because there is no efficient chain of devolution between them and those at the top.

The pace and degree of Africanisation differ in the various countries. But in all it is conspicuous. This, in general, is not because the expatriates, as had sometimes been feared, were not prepared to stay or because the new regimes have pushed them out come what may. On

37 This inflation has hardly started in East Africa; maybe it will be avoided but if so I shall be surprised.

the contrary, there has been a remarkably smooth transition during which, in the words of Sir Ivor Jennings, "the Minister, who was yesterday a 'rabble-rousing agitator,' perhaps newly released from internment, and an official who was yesterday a 'lackey of imperialism' . . . work together in intimate harmony to build up a new nation."[38]

There are signs, however, that the basic principle of the Whitehall model, that the civil service should be insulated from politics, may not long survive. The public service commissions, which were intended to ensure this insulation, have been reduced to the level of merely advisory bodies in Ghana, Tanganyika and Uganda. In Tanganyika, President Nyerere has publicly expressed the view that in a one-party state it is wrong "to continue with the present artificial distinction between politicians and civil servants—a distinction desirable only in the context of a multi-party system where the continuity of public administration must not be thrown out of gear at every switch from one 'party' government to another."[39]

Hence, in Tanganyika, civil servants are under pressure to become members of TANU (the "one-party"). In Ghana, Nigeria, and Sierra Leone the present governments consist, in effect, of an alliance between the military and the civil services, and it is difficult to see how the latter can remain aloof from politics any more than the former. Indeed, in Nigeria at present it is the civil service, rather than the military, that is in command.

38 *Democracy in Africa* (Cambridge, Eng., 1963), p. 60.

39 "Democracy and the Party System," *Spearhead*, Vol. 1, No. 1 (1963), quoted by J. P. W. B. McAuslan (1964) 13 *ICLQ* 526. Still more extreme expressions of the same view were constantly voiced by the party press in Ghana; see W. B. Harvey, *Law and Social Change in Ghana* (Princeton, 1966), pp. 61-65.

In general, however, a distinction is still recognised between the (theoretically) changeable politicians or military commanders who determine policy, and the non-political permanent administrators who carry it out. The distinction is less clear-cut in local government. The British system of elected councils employing permanent officials rarely works efficiently on African soil and the tendency is for increasing control by administrators, who are also politicians, appointed by the central government.

Perhaps the most disturbing change has been the spread of corruption and nepotism. In West Africa traditional practices of the ubiquitous "dash" and of giving and receiving gifts for services sought and rendered have been debased into barefaced bribery and extortion, spreading throughout public life from the bottom almost to the top. These were always present but in colonial days rarely spread high up. Post-independence changes at the top have taken the lid off.

I do not suggest for one moment that African civil servants are inherently less honest than anyone else. But, as Mr. Chinua Achebe's novel *No Longer at Ease*[40] so brilliantly portrays, the African civil servant is subjected to demands and temptations not experienced by the expatriate. He is expected to help educate members of his extended family and to repay to the family or to the clan or village organisation the amount spent on his own education. He feels himself obliged to observe the old traditions of hospitality to kinsmen[41] and lavish expenditure on marriages and funerals, while yet

40 London, 1960. Also in (paperback) Heinemann's African Writers Series, 1963.

41 One of the great problems of mixed marriage is that the white spouse finds it difficult to adjust to a home life in which one or more of the "in-laws" is always in residence.

maintaining the standards of life expected of the new elite. And he is the legatee of the tradition established in colonial days that it was not immoral to cheat the government. The temptations and opportunities are great, the risk of detection relatively slight, and the moral stigma if found out not damning.

At the top, too, as has been clearly brought out in a number of recent investigations, corrupt payments are often extorted not so much for personal gain but to line the coffers of a political party.[42] Few African politicans would regard this as particularly reprehensible—if parties are necessary they have to be financed somehow, and bitter experience shows that membership fees do not suffice. In a one-party state, who, indeed, is hurt? If "Ghana was the C.P.P. and the C.P.P. was Ghana" did it matter how the price was divided between the government and the C.P.P.? It did, of course, if only because it meant that government contracts were awarded not on merit but to the contractor prepared to offer the largest bribe. Most expatriate firms, much to their discredit, were as ready to pay the bribes as were the ministers and officials to receive them.

Nepotism, too, is widespread and, here again, the moral sanctions against it are weak. Anyone who obtains a position in which he can find jobs for his kinsmen is expected to do so, and would lose face if he did not. The public service commissions are intended to guard against this, but, as we have seen, in some countries they have been emasculated. And everywhere, if a minister wants his girl-friend as his personal secretary

42 See, for example, the *Report of the Coker Commission of Inquiry into the Affairs of Certain Statutory Corporations in Western Nigeria* (Lagos: Federal Ministry of Information, 1962), and post-coup commissions of inquiry in Ghana and Nigeria.

or a lad from his village as his messenger, he will generally have his way. In local government, corruption and nepotism are at their worst. Bribery is widespread in the lower echelons of the police service and in some customary courts and even magistrates' courts. Yet there *are* uncorrupt African organisations such as the clan, district, and age-group organisations which perform such an important role in African life, and which appear to be virtually free from this vice. These and other indigenous institutions, such as the recognition of extended family obligations, provide a remarkable system of social security.[43] The tragedy is that the indigenous system has not been integrated with the Westernised administrative and economic organisation to which different standards are applied.

Opinions differ as to how important and how harmful the spreading corruption and nepotism are. The authors of a recent study conclude that by and large neither is worse than in Britain in the eighteenth and early nineteenth centuries.[44] We survived pretty well—and, in due course, eradicated them pretty effectively. Other modern states do pretty well without having eradicated them.[45] But if it be a fact, as it was widely believed to be in Nigeria, that every government contract cost the country at least 10 per cent more than it should because of bribes, this tax on the finances of

43 So remarkable that in the last half of 1966 refugees officially estimated to total upwards of one and a quarter million people have been quietly absorbed in Eastern Nigeria, notwithstanding that it is the most heavily populated region.

44 Ronald Wraith and Edgar Simpkins, *Corruption in Developing Societies* (London, 1963).

45 When some years ago I met a body of South African public accountants the main question they asked was what their duty was when they found items in the accounts which undoubtedly represented bribes to public servants. It was, they said, a constant worry.

poor countries is one which they can ill afford even if some of it finds its way into the coffers of their political parties.[46] What is most disturbing is that corruption, both petty and grand, has been growing not diminishing.[47] I cannot say from personal experience how far this applies to all the countries with which I am concerned. Until the recent coups it certainly applied in full measure to Nigeria and Ghana and, it is my impression, in some measure to all. It was clearly far less in high places in East, than in West Africa. In West Africa the new military regimes have declared their intention to eradicate it. It is to be hoped that they will succeed.

Another weakness of the Whitehall export model is its excessive reliance on tradition, individual rectitude, public opinion, and parliamentary questioning. In countries where these safeguards may not operate, a mere legacy of administrative fairness, even when buttressed by public service commissions, is an inadequate protection against administrative misbehaviour. The need has clearly been shown for legally enforceable rules of administrative conduct (as in the United States) and for an ombudsman (as in Scandinavia and New Zealand). Britain bequeathed neither because we had neither to bequeath.[48] Here again Tanganyika breaks new ground.

46 It would appear that the "official" ruling rate in Ghana was only 5 per cent; see the recently published *Report of the Commission to Inquire into the Affairs of NADECO Ltd.* (Accra, 1966).

47 A one-party political system probably encourages its growth. "If there is one danger of a single party system for all its obvious attractions to the new African leaders, it is that here, if anywhere, by the overwhelming testimony of history in every age and country, is the breeding place of corrupt influences which can spread poison through the whole bloodstream of society." Hunter, *New Societies*, p. 236.

48 An ombudsman bill, the Parliamentary Commissioner Bill, is at present before the British Parliament. The independence constitution of Guyana does provide for an ombudsman.

The interim constitution for Tanzania[49] establishes a Permanent Commission of Enquiry which may inquire into the conduct of any official and shall so inquire if directed by the president. It will be interesting to see how effective this is and how far it is copied elsewhere (the appointment of a somewhat similar watchdog committee has just been announced in Ghana). Its obvious weakness, under a president less trustworthy than Nyerere, is its excessive subservience to the president. Its members are appointed by the president and to the president it reports without itself possessing any power of enforcing its recommendations. In the absence of an effective and independent legislature, it is questionable whether this suffices to prevent executive abuses.

Yet, despite everything, the civil service has perhaps proved the most valuable of all the British legacies. Without it Nigeria might already have gone the way of the Congo. The tragedy is that the Nigerian federal service is now being gravely weakened by the loss of hundreds of its best men, including many of those at the top.

7. *The Military and the Police*

Perhaps the most unexpected and ironical feature of post-independence experience has been the vital political role played, with varying success, by the army and, to a lesser extent, the police. The army mutinies in East Africa early in 1964 seem to have been due to nothing more serious than a temporary breakdown of discipline due to over-hasty Africanisation of the commissioned ranks and dissatisfaction with conditions of service. What, however, they did show was that, minute though the armies were, disaffection in their ranks

49 Act No. 43 of 1965, chap. vi.

could be suppressed only by calling in troops from outside. The lesson was not ignored by the political elites who took still more care to ensure that, as British officers were replaced, those who succeeded them were those on whose personal loyalty the political leaders thought they could rely. In Ghana, indeed, Nkrumah resorted to a series of purges and built up a personal bodyguard with Russian, rather than British, training.

A succession of crises in Nigeria culminated in 1965 in a breakdown of law and order throughout large areas of Yorubaland and total disillusionment among the educated classes throughout the country.[50] In January, 1966 certain army officers of the rank of major and below staged a coup. It seems clear that their seniors were not parties to this and that, indeed, the plan was to assassinate them together with the more important political leaders. The plan partly misfired, except in the north, but in the absence of the prime minister, who was among the victims, there was no one with sufficient influence in a deeply divided council of ministers to secure agreement to calling in British troops as Nyerere had done in Tanganyika. Instead they handed over power to General Aguiyi-Ironsi, the Army Commander, and he had to make terms with the leaders of the coup and, in effect, to assume the leadership of the revolt. Shortly afterwards the army in Ghana staged a successful coup against Nkrumah's regime—a coup which would have been bloodless but for the resistance of Nkrumah's body-

50 A good account of these will be found in Mackintosh, *Nigerian Government and Politics*, chap. iii; and in F. A. O. Schwarz, *Nigeria: The Tribes, the Nation, or the Race—The Politics of Independence* (Cambridge, Mass., 1965). For rival accounts of subsequent developments, see *Nigeria 1966* (Lagos, Federal Ministry of Information, 1967) and *Nigerian Crisis 1966* (4 vols.; Enugu, Eastern Nigerian Ministry of Information, 1967).

guard. Within a month rumours broke out of a threatened military coup in Uganda. On this occasion, however, the army eventually supported the prime minister who, with their aid, was able to resolve the long-standing rivalry between himself and the president, the Kabaka, by ousting the latter, and thereafter to secure the adoption of a new constitution which greatly reduced the autonomy of Buganda. In March 1967 the army seized power in Sierra Leone.

In these countries the army has proved to be the political *deus ex machina*—hardly the role intended for it by those who nurtured it so carefully in the nonpolitical British tradition. On the other hand, it can be said that in all the ex-British African countries the army has shown itself to be the least tribalistic of all the indigenous power groups. The coups which it staged in Nigeria and Ghana appear to have been responsive to public opinion, to have been mounted as a last resort when constitutional changes had been shown to be impossible, and to have been potentially beneficial. To that extent the army has in fact lived up to its traditions by placing national needs above those of party, tribe, or faction. Unfortunately it is not easy to find similar justification for the latest military coup in Sierra Leone. There internal army rivalries appear to have played a major role and to have led to the premature destruction of democratic institutions which had just proved themselves capable of working better than most had expected.

Both in Nigeria and Ghana the military leaders have displayed what appears to be a sincere wish to be relieved of the duties of government as soon as a viable civilian regime can be established. Ghana is less tribally divided than Nigeria (this was one of Nkrumah's genuine achievements), and there effective civilian rule of some sort should be relatively easy to re-establish; steps in this direction seem to be proceeding reasonably smoothly. Nigeria's tragedy is that the tribal rivalries have now split the army itself and bid fair to destroy the country. The coup left in the saddle not those who had planned it, but some of its intended victims. The politicians who had chosen General Aguiyi-Ironsi as Army Commander were probably right in thinking that he was not the stuff of which revolutionaries were made. He did not give the incisive leadership which, in the euphoric atmosphere of January, might perhaps have succeeded in welding Nigeria into one nation under a unitary constitution. Later attempts to scrap regionalism incited a further outburst of tribal feeling which spread to the army itself. By July the northerners had persuaded themselves that the original coup was an eastern Ibo plot against them,[51] and northern soldiers took their revenge by shooting most of the remaining Ibo officers. That effectively ended a unified military command.

The government, now as weak and divided as had been the civilian federal government that it replaced, released the politicians with a view to handing back the reins to them. But while desperate attempts were being made to devise a constitution which would restore some measure of mutual confidence, further outbreaks of violence constantly occurred and those in the north in September amounted to a large scale massacre of Ibos in which bands of undisciplined soldiers participated. Army units had to be re-deployed so that they were serving in their own tribal areas[52]—an open recognition that the army was no longer capable of acting as a united

51 Just as many Ibos were persuaded that the January coup had only just forestalled a northern-inspired revolt in the East.

52 Except that northern soldiers have had to be kept in Lagos.

or unifying force. Although police discipline had been generally maintained—a superb achievement—the unarmed police were unable to guarantee protection to minorities, and massive repatriation of populations took place with lamentable consequences, both human and economic.

Nigeria is now on the brink of splitting into two or more parts—indeed, effectively, the east is at present outside the federation. About the only remaining cohesive factors are the reluctance of the other regions to lose the oil wells in the east; the fact that many of these wells are in minority areas in the east; the vast numbers of Ibos who worked in regions other than their homeland, the east; the vital role they played in trade and communications in the north; and the difficulty that the east will find in absorbing all of them if they return permanently. These considerations of self-interest are coupled with a widespread feeling that if Nigeria disintegrates she will have failed not only herself but the whole of black Africa. On these crumbling foundations the few untarnished statesmen with vision and ideals are striving to rebuild and re-unite their potentially great country. Whether they can succeed time alone will tell. What is certain is that English-speaking Africa's first taste of military rule has turned very sour. Unfortunately this has not deterred others from resorting to the rule of force.

8. *The Rule of Law*

I described the rule of law as only indirectly a legacy of colonialism. But it is regarded by many nationalist leaders as a colonial legacy; and this is unfortunate for they associate it with colonialism and imperialism and are suspicious of it. That may be one reason why it has not fared as well as had been hoped.

It suffered most in Ghana where latterly the Nkrumah regime displayed a neurotic suspicion of the law, lawyers and, above all, judges, who were regarded as innately subversive of the C.P.P. Despite the wish for a legally enforceable bill of rights, which had been expressed at the time of independence, none was, in fact, incorporated in Ghana's post-independence republican constitution. Instead the president, on assuming office, was required to make a solemn declaration affirming his adherence to certain fundamental principles. The Ghana supreme court held, inevitably, that this imposed merely moral obligations on him and did not restrict his or the legislature's legal powers.[53] Preventive detention, without trial or other safeguards, was introduced and detainees denied any resort to the courts. The judicial service commission was abolished even prior to the introduction of the republican constitution, and, subsequently, the president was accorded unfettered powers over judicial appointments and dismissals and exercised this power to fire certain judges.[54] By retroactive legislation he was also given power to declare the decision of a court in a criminal matter to be of no effect,[55] and exercised this too. It can be strongly argued that this last power was unconstitutional, as vesting a judicial power in the executive, but it was not challenged—an illustration of the growing atrophy of the rule of law. Since it was these abuses that contributed to Nkrumah's downfall it is to be hoped that the new regime will extirpate

[53] *Re Akoto* (1961), Civil Appeal No. 42.

[54] He had earlier dismissed the Chief Justice from that appointment after an unpopular verdict in a trial for a political offence and secured his resignation from the bench. In contrast with the British convention, judges who had resigned or been dismissed were permitted to return to practice (but not to appear in court); see *Judicial Service (Amendment) Act*, 1964 (Act 245).

[55] *Criminal Procedure (Amendment) (No. 2) Act, 1963* (Act 223).

them. Although it has repealed the Preventive Detention Act, initially it detained about as many people as it released, but this, perhaps, was to be expected and condoned under emergency conditions and most have now been set free. It has already restored the judicial service commission—though as an advisory body only—and has carried out a pretty thorough purge of the bench, which Nkrumah had begun to pack.

The position is not wholly reassuring in Tanganyika; it, too, has no bill of rights, has introduced preventive detention, and has curtailed the powers of the judicial service commission. On the other hand, detainees are afforded greater safeguards, at least on paper. And although judges are appointed by the president they cannot be dismissed except, in the case of the High Court, on a report by a committee of which a majority must be judges, and in the case of the lower magistracy by the judicial service commission.[56] President Nyerere's reproof to those who criticised as excessively lenient the sentences passed on the army mutineers was a reassuring token of his determination to preserve judicial independence. He pointed out that any attempt to interfere with the sentences would abrogate the very rule of law for breach of which the soldiers had been condemned.[57] This is a refreshing contrast with the actions of the former president of Ghana. Equally reassuring is the creation of the ombudsman commission to which I have already referred. But the position in Zanzibar, the other part of the so-called United Republic of Tanzania, is more disturbing.

[56] *Interim Constitution*, No. 43 of 1965, s. 58 and s. 61. S. 61 does not apply to Zanzibar.

[57] See *Bulletin of the International Commission of Jurists*, No. 20 (September 1964), p. 49.

In Nigeria, the judicial service commissions were abolished both at the regional and federal levels and the directors of public prosecutions were deprived of their independent status and made subject to the control of the attorneys general. But Nigeria still retains her bill of rights and has not resorted to preventive detention except under emergency conditions, which, of course, prevail at present. As in Ghana, the military regime has already reestablished an advisory judicial service committee.

Uganda resolved its recent crisis and promulgated a new constitution in a way which, even if it complied with the letter of the law, was hardly in accordance with its spirit. However, the new constitution retains the original bill of rights and safeguards for judicial independence, though the director of public prosecutions becomes subject to the control of the attorney general. Kenya, though in many ways an amazing success story in the light of its troubled years immediately before independence, has recently passed a constitutional amendment which permits legislation providing for preventive detention and restriction to be introduced on the order of the president. The order lapses after 28 days unless approved by a parliamentary resolution and cannot last for more than eight months unless extended by a like resolution. But while it is in force nothing contained in or done under the legislation is to be regarded as inconsistent with the fundamental rights of personal liberty and non-discrimination, freedom from arbitrary search, or freedom of expression, assembly, and movement. The safeguards for the independence of judges and the attorney general still remain.

In Sierra Leone the proposed republican constitution retains the bill of rights but demotes the judicial service commission so that its powers of appointment relate only to subordinate judicial officers; superior judges are to be appointed by the president on the advice of the cabinet and removed if a two-thirds majority of all the members of parliament so resolve because of the judge's inability to act or misbehaviour. The introduction of this new constitution has been aborted by the military coup but the existing constitution has been suspended. Only the Gambia, which has just achieved independence, has not yet made any inroads into the initial safeguards.

What of the future? Apart from Malawi,[58] all the countries which started independence with bills of rights still retain them; even under the military regime in Nigeria fundamental rights have not been formally suspended, though military decrees cannot be attacked in the courts. They are proud of them: like airlines and television services, they are prestigious things to have. Moreover, in countries with serious minority problems they are rightly regarded as an essential element in the protection of these minorities. How far these considerations will guarantee their survival depends mainly, as it seems to me, upon how constraining the bills of rights prove to be. If they are constantly invoked and if the courts apply them robustly, thus preventing the governments from doing what they want to do, they will either be abolished in toto, or whittled away, or, what might be worst, the bench will be packed with judges that the governments think they can trust not to be robust.

58 The comprehensive bill of rights in the independence constitution is scrapped in the 1966 republican constitution. Certain fundamental principles are stated but no law is invalidated thereby if it was reasonably required in the interests of defence, public safety, or public order. For a description of the new constitution, see Simon Roberts in [1966] Public Law 304.

That may seem a harsh thing to say, but I think it is at present the only realistic answer. Politicians in Africa, as elsewhere, constantly express a devotion to the rule of law (or to Socialist Legality), but their devotion wanes if it prevents them from doing what they want. Resentment at being "dragged to court" and hostility to the courts when they put a spoke in the wheel were felt not only in Ghana in the days when Dr. Danquah harassed the C.P.P. government. They were felt and expressed just as strongly by responsible and respected statesmen in Nigeria, from the prime minister downwards, when the Supreme Court enjoined the inquiry into the National Bank, and when the Privy Council held that Chief Akintola had been validly removed from the premiership of the Western Region.[59] The fact is that respect for the rule of law and for the courts is not yet, in these countries, sufficiently deep-rooted to survive any exercise of the courts' powers which prevented a government from taking a course of action which it thought necessary.

Probably these bills of rights would never have been adopted at all if they had not been so qualified that they almost appear, as has been said, to be "bills of exceptions rather than bills of rights." Had they followed the United States' model they might, as Dean Griswold suggested in his Maccabaean Lecture, have had greater emotional appeal.[60] But the African courts

[59] *Doherty v. Balewa* (1961), All N.L.R. 604. affd. sub. nom. *Balewa* v. *Doherty* [1963] 1 W.L.R. 949, P.C. See the quotations in O. I. Odumosu, *The Nigerian Constitution: History and Development* (London, 1963), pp. 299-301. The Akintola litigation is contained in *Adegbenro* v. *Akintola* [1963] A.C. 614, P.C. This decision was immediately reversed by a retrospective amendment of the constitution.

[60] Erwin N. Griswold, "Two Branches of the Same Stream," the Third Maccabaean Lecture in Jurisprudence, London, October 18, 1962.

do not yet possess the aura of sanctity which your Supreme Court enjoys, and the African governments would not have been prepared to entrust them with the same discretions. The exceptions had to be spelled out in advance, and to be sufficiently wide to enable the governments to preserve law and order and to build up their new nations. If they prove in fact to be too narrow or the courts too bold, not only will the bills of rights be in danger but so may the whole principle of judicial review of legislative and administrative action.[61]

Does this mean, then, that the bills of rights are useless? I do not think so. Their great value, as I see it, is that their mere presence exercises a restraining influence. In particular, they greatly strengthen the hands of the governments' legal advisers in their efforts to maintain the rule of law and respect for the individual. If a minister of justice or an attorney general can say to his cabinet colleagues: "Speaking as a lawyer it is my duty to advise you that you can't do that,"[62] it is infinitely more effective than if he can only say: "Speaking as a minister, I don't think we ought to do that." This emphasises how important the lawyer's role is in this field, and how vital it is that the legal professions should be imbued with a determination to maintain the rule of law and all the legal safeguards which protect it.

61 In other words, I believe that it was essential to incorporate those features of the fundamental rights provisions which make them distasteful to an American observer such as F. A. O. Schwarz: "The first reaction to the Nigerian fundamental rights provisions of one trained in the American tradition is to stress the negative—the dullness of the prolix language, the breadth of the exceptions, the ability of Parliament to change the rules of the game, and the somewhat hesitant attitude of the courts." *Nigeria*, p. 188.

62 As it is understood that the federal minister of justice told the Nigerian police when they wanted to tap the telephones of those suspected of complicity in the conspiracy that led to the conviction of the leaders of the Action Group.

If they are, these legal safeguards may acquire greater strength and the role of the courts greater veneration. At present, however, it would be foolish to pretend that either is not somewhat precarious.

It would also be foolish to pretend that the existence of a legally enforceable bill of rights in itself ensures the maintenance of the rule of law as we understand it—after all, Rhodesia has one. The exceptions to the legal safeguards are very wide—just how wide was shown when the Nigerian federal government was able, as a result of a disturbance in the Western Regional Parliament, to assume the government of the region and to introduce and exercise powers of preventive detention and restriction.[63] In any case there is a limit to the extent to which any legal rules and remedies can ensure political propriety: when candidates at the Nigerian federal election of December, 1964, alleged that their nomination papers had been suppressed or that they had been prevented from handing them in, they were understandably not placated by the bland reply that they had their remedy in the courts. Nevertheless that was the remedy to which they ultimately resorted. And that crisis in Nigeria was resolved on the advice of jurists not generals. The rule of law triumphed, but it had been subjected to a greater strain than it should have been called upon to bear. A year later it broke beneath the strain and it was the generals not the jurists who triumphed.

That so many of these countries resort to preventive detention is, perhaps, the development that has caused

[63] The *locus standi* rule is another factor which significantly restricts the effectiveness of the rights. To test the validity of a ban on political meetings it is necessary to hold a meeting and risk being sent to gaol.

most concern—and understandably so. But it was, surely, too much to hope for anything else. The British, after all, did not succeed in ruling most of these countries without preventive detention[64] and the new rulers do not feel themselves any more secure. One sometimes feels that they exaggerate their insecurity and that, as in the early days of Ghana, it was repression that led to disaffection rather than disaffection which led to, and justified, repression. But disaffection there certainly has been: plots everywhere, mutinies in Kenya, Uganda, and Tanganyika; and successful coups d'etat in Zanzibar, Nigeria, Ghana, Sierra Leone, and (arguably) Uganda. The situation in surrounding territories has been even worse: successful coups d'etat in Togo, Dahomey, Congo-Brazzaville, the Central African Republic, Upper Volta, Gabon, Burundi, and the Sudan; civil war in Congo-Kinshasa; sabotage in the Cameroons; genocide in Ruanda; and assassination (of two prime ministers) in Burundi.[65] In these circumstances it is hardly surprising that the governments have protected themselves with the shield that the colonialists taught them to use.

One further point should be mentioned in this connection. I have long wondered whether one aspect of the Anglo-American method of maintaining the rule of law does not actually encourage a resort to preventive detention—the negation of the rule of law. I refer to our "accusatorial" criminal trial, and the extreme protection afforded the accused. The excuse always given

64 But, in recent years, only after the declaration of a state of emergency.

65 This incomplete catalogue makes Africa sound terribly dangerous. Yet when one is there it seems much more friendly and less dangerous than Central Park or Boston Common.

for resorting to preventive detention is: "We know these chaps are plotting but we can't prove it in court." The orthodox reply is: "If you can't prove it in court, you can't be sure." But is that true? And even if it is, does one have to be absolutely sure before taking preventive action to preserve the security of the state? Under the continental inquisitorial system would it not be much easier to become sure one way or the other, and to prove guilt if guilt there be? Do the French territories, for this reason, find it less necessary to resort to preventive detention? I do not know the answers to these questions. So far as I am aware, no empirical research has been done to find the answers. I wish someone would undertake it.

Another disturbing feature is the trend towards the abolition of judicial service commissions and the other safeguards of judicial independence.[66] The primary reason for this, in my opinion, is not so much that the governments wish to make political appointments to, or dismissals from, the bench, but rather their resentment at the implied suggestion that they cannot be trusted as much as the British not to do so.[67] Unfor-

66 The recent partial restoration of these safeguards in Nigeria and Ghana is not enough, in my view, to be sure that this trend has been reversed. Recent developments in those countries may account for the fact that Sierra Leone dropped the proposal to become a *de jure* one-party state, but they did not lead to the preservation of the original safeguards of judicial independence in the proposed republican constitution.

67 Other reasons that have been advanced against judicial service commissions are: (1) the delays which occur if an appointment has to be made during the long vacation when the chairman (the chief justice) is likely to be on leave; (2) the fact that the commission may be as prone to favouritism (though perhaps of a different type) as the government, (e.g., the local bench and bar may want "jobs for the [indigenous] boys" when an exclusion of expatriates is premature); and (3) that appointments by committees tend to represent the highest common factor of general agreement and therefore to go to pedestrian characters to whom nobody objects.

tunately, conditions in Africa are not comparable with those in Britain, where a non-political tradition has been established, where the dominant voice in judicial appointments is that of the Lord Chancellor's Department—a department singularly aloof from political pressures, and where Parliament has never exercised its powers of dismissal. Some of the appointments and dismissals recently made in the African countries (and I am not thinking only of Ghana) do not inspire confidence in the protestation that political considerations will be eschewed.

Fortunately, as experience in South Africa (and, may I add, the United States?) has shown, even political appointees generally respond to the atmosphere of the judicial bench, and manfully suppress their political prejudices and any desire to ingratiate themselves with their appointors. It may be surmised, however, that not all would succeed if they knew that they risked losing their jobs if they did. The East African countries, including Tanganyika, still retain adequate legal safeguards for judicial security of tenure. In West Africa they are disappearing, and it is greatly to be hoped that the promised new constitutions will effectively restore them. One can, of course, make an argument for the proposition that, having regard to the judges' law-making role, political considerations should not be wholly eschewed and that it is legitimate to appoint a judge because his views are in accord with the basic ideology of the government or to dismiss him if it is obvious that they are not. Unhappily, events in Africa and elsewhere suggest that powers vested in politicians will all too often be exercised for less worthy political motives; a man will be appointed to the bench to make a vacancy for another in his present political post, or dismissed because the government does not approve of his refusal to substitute expediency for justice.

The removal of the independence of the director of public prosecutions is of less moment. The original rules were somewhat unrealistic, for prosecutions are inevitably liable to raise political issues, both domestic and international—as Britain found when she prosecuted a Russian athlete for allegedly stealing a dollar hat from a self-service store. It was, indeed, the narrow avoidance of a diplomatic incident that led Nigeria to make this change.

Reviewing the future of the rule of law in Africa in the light of developments up to date it is impossible to feel confident. Legal safeguards are diminishing and actual practice is disturbing. Perhaps as disturbing as the more highly publicised tendencies to which I have referred is the harassing and bullying which a semi-illiterate population are apt to suffer at the hands of the police. Actual "third-degree" methods may be no more common than in Britain, but cat-and-mouse tactics certainly are—at any rate in West Africa. People against whom any complaint has been made are forced to report daily to the police station for weeks or months while investigations (allegedly) continue. Sometimes this is due to mere incompetence; more often, probably, in the hope of extracting a bribe. This and other malpractices will not be eradicated until the quality of the police is improved and until there is a stronger legal profession and adequate arrangements are made (effectively there are none at present) for legal aid for the indigent.

There is, however, one redeeming and reassuring feature of the present situation: there *is* an informed public opinion in these countries, and, within limits, it is allowed to express itself. The limits appear to be contracting because of over-sensitivity to criticism and because a feeling of insecurity often leads governments to invoke sedition acts which they themselves had attacked in colonial days, and to invoke them against newspaper articles which the colonial governments would, I think, have condoned. They have also led to a discernible tendency towards increased press censorship. Happily, one of the lessons which African leaders should now have learned is that, if the limits of permissible criticism contract too far, informed public opinion will make itself felt nonetheless.

9. *The Common Law Legacy*

I can dispose more rapidly of what I described as the common law legacy because in the field of law reform disappointingly little has been done since independence. Some progress has been made with the integration of the customary courts into a unified court structure; much has been done to complete the Africanisation of the bench. But little effort has been made to grapple with the other tasks that lie ahead.

As I see it, these tasks are: first, to ensure that the law applying in these countries is more readily accessible than in alien (English) statute books and law reports; ideally the accessible form should be local codes. Second, to adapt the received English law so as to make it really applicable to local conditions and ideologies; unless and until the whole law is codified this means giving judges freedom to develop a judge-made law which does not slavishly follow English decisions and ensuring that the judges are equipped for that role. Third, to bring about greater unification between divergent customary laws and between them and English law. Fourth, as a long-term aim, to do away altogether with the dichotomy between the received English law and customary law, and in the meantime to reform those aspects of customary law, especially in the fields of land law and inheritance, which inhibit economic growth. These are mammoth tasks, and the last cannot be completely accomplished so long as the subsistence sector of the economy continues. They demand the services of highly skilled lawyers, who are capable of undertaking research in conjunction with anthropologists, sociologists, and economists. These lawyers must have a sound knowledge of the laws of their own countries, customary law included, and of legal developments elsewhere. They must be highly competent legal draftsmen, able to translate the results of their researches into clear and workable codes. And, above all, they must be lawyers who recognise the need for law reform and do not think, as so many appear to at present, that everything in their legal garden is lovely and that English law represents the perfection of human reason.

In West Africa only Ghana has made any real start on any of these tasks. There a programme of reform and codification was instituted, especially in the field of company and commercial law—an ironical adjunct to an economic and political policy which did not encourage private enterprise. Ghana also amended the statutory formula regulating the reception of English law so as to free her judges from the need slavishly to follow English decisions and so as to encourage the assimilation of customary and received law. She clarified the rules for ascertaining customary law and resolving internal conflicts and, following the earlier example of Western Nigeria, embarked on a programme of re-enactment, with amendments, of the statutes of general application.[68] But despite her protestations she did little to adapt the common law to the specific needs of an African society let alone to "African socialism." One of the great challenges to the common lawyer in Africa is how to adjust the common law to such a society without destroying its humanistic core.

The other West African countries can hardly be said to have started on any of these tasks. The inactivity of Nigeria is particularly disappointing for she, after Ghana, has had the longest time and has by far the largest legal profession.

In East Africa useful activity has taken place toward codifying and unifying the customary laws.[69] Unification has gone furthest in Tanganyika. The ultimate objective is the production of a series of declarations in codified form covering all the main fields (except land law) in which customary law is important. Draft declarations of customary laws are submitted to a panel of experts and then to district councils. Efforts are made to iron out differences so as to obtain unified declarations applying as widely as possible. When general agreement is obtained a government notice is published declaring the unified law as stated in the declaration to be the customary law throughout the area to which it relates.

68 For a good short description of the matters dealt with in this paragraph, see F. A. R. Bennion, *The Constitutional Law of Ghana* (London, 1962), chaps. x-xii.

69 For an account of these developments see W. L. Twining, *The Place of Customary Law in the National Legal Systems of East Africa* (Chicago, 1964); and the *Report of the African Conference on Local Courts and Customary Law*, Dar es Salaam, September 8-18, 1963 (Dar es Salaam: Faculty of Law, University College, 1963); and E. Cotran, "The Place and Future of Customary Law in East Africa," in *East African Law Today* (British Institute of International and Comparative Law, Commonwealth Law Series No. 5; London, 1966), p. 72.

Closely related to the Tanganyikan project is that for the Restatement of African Law instituted in 1959 by the School of Oriental and African Studies of the University of London. This aims at producing written restatements of the customary laws of no less than sixteen countries in English-speaking Africa. So far it has made most progress in Kenya where a restatement of customary criminal laws has already been produced. This has shown that most customary offences are already covered by the Penal Code and that, if a few additions were made to the Code, customary criminal law could be abolished there as it already has been in most of the other countries. First drafts of a restatement of matrimonial law have also been completed, but so far as this and other branches of civil law are concerned, there is no immediate intention of giving the restatements binding force or of deliberately producing uniformity. The idea is that, like the American restatements, they shall be of persuasive authority only. In fact, however, they will differ fundamentally from the American model because, apart from court records and the odd book by an anthropologist, they will constitute the only written sources of customary law and inevitably, therefore, will carry great weight.

Unfortunately, this restatement project has aroused little enthusiasm in East Africa and even less in West Africa. Many lawyers take the view that the best thing that can happen to customary laws is their speedy disappearance, and they are suspicious of anything that might give them a new lease of life. My own view is that the disappearance of customary laws is dependent upon the disappearance of the subsistence sector and that, even then, the demise of customary law without a radical Africanisation of the received English law would be a tragedy. So long as customary laws remain, there is everything to be said for making them more readily ascertainable in written restatements. And this will inevitably lead toward greater unification, whether that is consciously aimed at or not.

The main lack everywhere, as I see it, is real effort toward adapting the received English law and local statute law to local conditions. At present the tendency is to Anglicise customary law rather than to Africanise English law. The integration of the customary courts into the common law system inevitably aggravates this tendency since the judges, even if they are Africans, will know much more English law than customary law and judges invariably tend to apply the legal system that they know.[70] This tendency is increased when judges of the customary courts themselves receive some training and supervision, as most now do, from lawyers with a common law training. It will become stronger still when qualified lawyers are appointed as customary court judges and legal representation is allowed—a development which has already occurred in some customary courts and which will inevitably spread.

Two further developments should here be referred to which theoretically might help to counteract this tendency. The British Institute of International and Comparative Law, with the encouragement of the British government and financial help from foundations, has instituted a service designed to assist African and other

70 It is a myth that African judges are likely to be much better informed on, or in sympathy with, customary laws than expatriates; recent experience suggests, in fact, that expatriates are more tender toward customary law than African lawyers who tend to despise it as primitive. See, for example, *Dawodu* v. *Danmole* [1962] 1 W.L.R. 1053, P.C., in which the African judge had thought the customary law rule to be contrary to natural justice, but the expatriate judges and the Privy Council decided that it was not.

Commonwealth countries to obtain expert assistance in connection with law reform projects and to obtain information about reforms taking place elsewhere.[71] But while this is undoubtedly worthwhile it is perhaps more probable that reform projects by British-trained experts will enhance the tendency towards Anglicisation rather than Africanisation.[72] These countries clearly need a more adequate machinery for law reform; but advice—however well-meaning and well-informed—is an adjunct to, not a substitute for, machinery.

The other development is the abolition of appeal to the Judicial Committee of the Privy Council by the states which have become republics.[73] Its disappearance, though regretted by many, including many African judges, seems inevitable throughout Africa.[74] This may

71 Very recently, a more elaborate scheme has been organised under U.N. auspices, the International Juridical Organisation for Developing Countries, with headquarters at Rome. Presumably too, the Commission of African Jurists established under O.A.U. auspices might play a role here. There is an obvious danger of unnecessary and wasteful diversity of effort.

72 There are many examples of this tendency, e.g., the introduction into Western Nigeria of the English Property Legislation of 1925, and the introduction in Kenya and Uganda of the English law of contract in place of the Indian Contract Act—which, if not specifically African, was at least an attempt to make English law more suitable for an underdeveloped country.

73 It seems to have been thought that republican status was inconsistent with appeal to the Privy Council. This is clearly incorrect. There would have been no difficulty in adapting the system which prevails in appeals from Malaysia under which the Judicial Committee "humbly advise" the head of state rather than Her Majesty. In fact the independence constitutions of Kenya, Malawi, and Zambia provided for appeal to the Judicial Committee as such.

74 The interest that is now being expressed in a peripatetic Commonwealth Court with a genuinely Commonwealth membership has come far too late to be practical politics. Yet some court aloof from internal tensions and tribal rivalries would be particularly valuable to the African states. The East Africa Court of Appeals still survives but there is no appeal to it on constitutional questions, where one would have thought it most needed. The West Africa Court of Appeals

at least encourage local judges to develop an indigenous case law which does not slavishly follow English decisions. That, however, requires a change of heart and in some countries, probably, a further change of law. At present it would be unthinkable for an African court to announce, as has the Australian High Court, that it does not propose to follow a House of Lords' decision.[75] Incidentally, it would also need a great improvement in the standards of local law reports, which at present are often years in arrear.

10. *The Economic Legacy*

In dealing with my tenth legacy, the economic one, I am not going to attempt to survey the economic development or stagnation of these countries since independence. All I need do is to draw attention to certain matters which directly affect the legal profession.

As I indicated in my first lecture, these countries were underdeveloped in the strictest sense. They still are. On the other hand they are striving to build up indigenous industry and commerce and to loosen the ties that bind these to the former colonial power. They regard the present situation as economic colonialism and are determined to rid themselves of it—without always heeding the advice of the economists that they cannot do so with-

---

has disappeared and there seems to be no chance of its revival. One day, perhaps, the O.A.U. will be able to establish a Pan-African supreme court; the example of the Canadian Supreme Court proves that it is not impossible to have a single court at the apex of common law and civil law jurisdictions.

[75] See *Parker* v. *The Queen* [1963] C.L.R. 610. The rejected decision of the House of Lords was in the much criticized *D.P.P.* v. *Smith* [1961] A.C. 290, a decision which was followed in 1961 with "respectful approval" by the supreme court of Ghana—then the least respectful of the African countries; see *Republic* v. *Tene Dagarti,* January-June, 1961, Cyclostyled Judgments (Criminal) 48.

out first increasing agricultural productivity. With the Eastern bloc eager to conclude trade agreements, it has not been difficult somewhat to alter the pattern of trade so that exports and imports are less exclusively to and from Britain; Ghana went some way in this direction, albeit with unhappy results to her economy since it led her to exchange the cocoa that she might have sold in world markets for goods that she did not need. Nigeria asserted her independence of Britain in a different way; she concluded an agreement of association with the European Common Market.

Increasingly in all countries expatriate interests are being ousted from the fields of retail trade and produce marketing, though the Asian grip on trade still remains strong in East Africa. Greater difficulty has been experienced in building up indigenous industrial enterprises. So far, the main progress has been through public rather than private effort. Projects have been handled either exclusively by the governments, often with massive financial aid from the World Bank or the like, or as joint efforts of the governments and foreign firms. The operation of many of these enterprises has not been wholly successful and has often led to grave scandals. Few of the reports of the frequent inquiries into their working were published, but one that was, painted a picture of graft and inefficiency which is probably all too typical.[76] Nevertheless, these public and semi-public enterprises have achieved more than indigenous private enterprise. Such factors as lack of capital or credit, a reluctance to combine resources, and the system of inheritance which sometimes inhibits the survival of a business for more

[76] *Report of the Coker Commission of Inquiry into the Affairs of Certain Statutory Corporations in Western Nigeria* (Lagos: Federal Ministry of Information, 1962). In Nigeria and Ghana post-coup reports are now emerging which more than confirm the picture.

than one generation, have combined to retard development even in the sphere of simple trading.[77]

The lesson for the legal profession seems clear. Competent commercial lawyers are needed, first to draw up the often extremely complicated legal agreements when a joint enterprise is launched, and second, as house-counsel or otherwise, to keep the public or semi-public corporations on the right course.[78] They are also needed to aid and guide the indigenous businessman and to help him to make best use of the organisational framework which the law provides. They are needed to help to adapt to African conditions the English-style company, partnership, and co-operative, and to evolve new types of organisation which may be better suited to local conditions and ideas.[79] Property lawyers are needed to help the African entrepreneur to make effective use of his resources so as to raise capital or obtain credit. Perhaps most of all they are needed to suggest reforms of land laws which in many parts of Africa are so complicated as virtually to take land, the African's main asset, out of economic circulation and to inhibit its productive capacity.[80]

77 For a good account of the difficulties faced by African enterprises, see Hunter, *The New Societies*, chap. vii. There is also the question of temperament: "Perhaps instinctively African leaders incline towards the State-run economy as against competitive free enterprise, knowing that their peoples have neither the taste nor the capacity for this extreme of individualism and personal dedication to an economic aim" (*ibid.*, p. 325).

78 The Volta Dam scheme involved well over one hundred agreements of fiendish difficulty. The lawyers who handled the matter were, almost exclusively, expatriates.

79 For an attempt in relation to companies and partnerships, see my *Final Report on the Company Law of Ghana* (Accra, 1961). The recommended Companies Code, Incorporated Private Partnerships Act, and Bodies Corporate (Official Liquidations) Act have since been enacted.

80 In an African culture, land is, of course, far more than a mere

11. *The Emotional and Moral Legacy*

Here again I can be brief since I have already covered incidentally most of what needs to be said. The moral aftermath of colonialism has been clearly reflected in the spread of corruption, in the self-aggrandisement of ministers and officials, and in a continued reluctance to co-operate with the police. The emotional legacy (colonial neurosis) still tends to inhibit an objective appraisal of past events or current needs.[81] It is also seen, to quote Frank Sutton's phrase, in "emotionally tinged acts and assertions that plainly affirm independence."[82] There have been examples of these in the legal field, such as the expulsion from Nigeria of an English Queen's Counsel (Mr. Dingle Foot, now the English Solicitor-General), and the refusal to allow another (Mr. E. F. N. Gratiaen) to enter the country to defend Chief Awolowo in the treason-felony trial. That incident may also illustrate the symptom of hypersensitivity to criticism, for the reason I was given for the expulsion of Mr. Foot was that on a previous visit to Nigeria, "he had called our prime minister a liar." As I understand it, all he had done was to deny, on the instructions of his client, the truth of certain statements made in an affidavit of the prime minister.

It seems to me, however, that what is really remark-

---

economic asset. But the fact that it is something more ought not to mean that it cannot be used as an economic asset at all.

81 It may even affect the balance of academic writings. Cf., for example, the critical account of the University of Ibadan (a colonial foundation) and the paean of praise of the University of Nigeria, Nsukka (a post-colonial foundation) in Ikejiani (ed.), *Nigerian Education,* pp. 138-70. Much of the criticism and much of the praise is entirely justified, but the impression given, that Ibadan was beset by constant strife whereas Nsukka was a trouble-free success story, could hardly be more misleading.

82 In Tilman and Cole, *Nigerian Political Scene,* p. 283.

able is how few such "emotionally tinged acts and assertions" there have been. How natural it would have been to take the pants off the white man—literally or metaphorically—as the Japanese did literally when they captured Shanghai. Nothing of the sort has occurred in anglophonic Africa. How natural it would have been to deport expatriates who had held powerful positions (for example, in the police or military) during the colonial regime. But the number who have been deported for no better reason could be counted on the fingers of one hand.[83] Nigeria, though she expelled Mr. Foot, and, for a time, would not let foreign lawyers in, ultimately permitted British lawyers to defend Chief Enahoro. Two of those whom Dr. Nkrumah deported from Ghana were shortly afterwards invited back by him—a remarkable example, surely, of pride swallowing. And a former boss of the United Africa Company (those notorious "colonial exploiters") who had left on retirement was asked to return to run one of the government boards. Whatever disturbances may have occurred since independence and however high tribal feelings may have run, no violence has been offered to expatriates and warring factions have combined to preserve their safety.

These are countries where for decades the white man assumed a position of superiority, treated Africans as inferior beings and made them feel that they were inferior. These are the countries whose inhabitants were the victims of the slave trade, that "unalleviated, unquestionable, widespread, long-continuing and highly-profitable crime" (the phrase is Margery Perham's[84])—a crime in which my country and yours were the princi-

83 A number of journalists have been expelled but that is rather an illustration of the sensitivity to criticism.

84 *The Colonial Reckoning* (London, 1961), p. 105.

pals. Who could have expected anything but bitter and aggressive acts of revenge and self-assertion? Yet how few these have been. This, surely, is the outstanding example of the maturity and the charity of those who now rule in our stead. Should we have behaved as well if the roles had been reversed? Will those who are still denied their independence because their white rulers refuse to bow to the "winds of change," behave as well when the inevitable break comes at last? These are uncomfortable questions which it behoves us to ask, but which I, fortunately, do not have to try to answer.

III

The Legal Profession

In the preceding lectures I attempted to describe some of the legacies left by Britain to her former dependencies in tropical Africa and to assess what is now happening to those legacies. Before dealing with my final legacy —the legal profession—let me try to summarise the reasons why these countries particularly need an adequate number of competent, courageous, and imaginative lawyers.

Before some audiences it might be necessary to justify the need for lawyers at all. Happily, speaking at the Harvard Law School, I can dispense with that. But the theme of these lectures is that the newly independent African states have an especial need for lawyers, and for lawyers who are something more than journeymen practitioners. The present state of the law itself creates this need, for, as I have tried to explain, the legal systems of these countries present peculiar complications and are in urgent need of root-and-branch reform if they are to be adapted to local needs. Hence the lawyers of these countries must not only be competent to administer and operate the law as it now is, but equipped and willing to reform it. But the legal legacy is but one, and perhaps in the long view the least important reason why lawyers are needed. Each of my other legacies emphasises, I submit, that the public responsibilities of the legal profession are even greater in these countries than in more highly developed industrial states. They need commercial, corporation, and property lawyers if they are to achieve an economic take-off. They need bilingual international, comparative, and constitutional lawyers if they are to survive as states and to enter into the larger unions which Pan-African sentiment and economic development demand, and if the Commonwealth is to survive as a worthwhile multi-racial organisation. They need courageous lawyers with the highest ethical standards if the atrophy of the rule of law and of personal and academic freedom, and the corrosive growth of corruption, nepotism, and elitism are to be arrested, and if military and police power is to be kept within bounds. Most of all, perhaps, they need constitutional lawyers sophisticated in other disciplines if they are to find a viable substitute for the Westminster model of parliamentary democracy.

In saying all this I do not want to exaggerate. I am not one of those lawyers who think that lawyers are more important than medical practitioners, engineers, agriculturalists, businessmen, or school teachers. On the contrary I freely concede that these countries need far more of the latter. One of the criticisms of the British legacies is that they left most of these countries with far too few. Another is that in West Africa they have led to a disproportionate number of lawyers. As yet the disproportion is relative rather than absolute. Too great a proportion of highly trained talent is being siphoned off into the legal profession to the detriment of other skills. The time has not yet come, except perhaps in a few cities, when there are more lawyers than work for them to do. But that too is an imminent danger; and it is dangerous not only because it is a waste of scarce human resources but also because it could lead to a general lowering of professional standards. What these countries need is a relatively small number of good lawyers. I have heard it argued that no great harm is done if they also have a larger number of bad or indifferent ones, because the good will drive out the bad. Alas, it is my belief that in this field, Gresham's Law operates and the bad debases the good. In private practice a largely unsophisticated clientele is not able rapidly to distinguish the good lawyer from the bad; in the public service a lawyer has to be very bad indeed before he can be dismissed.

What I am arguing is that the medical practitioners, engineers, and the like will not be able to perform their even more vital tasks unless law and order are preserved in these countries; and they will not be preserved without an adequate number of first-rate lawyers. Indeed, I go further and contend that without strong legal professions these countries have little hope of solving their pressing problems or, indeed, of long-term survival as true democracies. This, as I see it, is the challenge which independent Africa presents to the legal profession. The remaining part of this lecture is devoted to the question whether the countries of ex-British tropical Africa presently have the sort of legal professions they need and what is being done to ensure that they shall have such professions in future.

1. *The British Legacy*

In all these countries the legal profession is based on the English model; as I said earlier this is one of the important legacies of British colonialism. In England the profession is divided into solicitors and barristers. This division was not adopted in any of the countries with which I am concerned; wisely, in my view, they followed the American example and all have a fused profession. Nevertheless, the British division has had most important and somewhat calamitous results in these African countries and I must say a word about it.[1]

The English division is based on two conventions: first, that the lay client has direct access to the solicitor only; and second, that the barrister alone has a right of audience in the superior courts. The practical consequences flowing from these conventions are that solicitors form the bulk of the profession; there are in England about 24,000 of them in practice and they are found throughout the length and breadth of the country. Normally, they practise in partnership and invariably they require a fairly elaborate office organisation. Since it is the solicitor to whom the layman is first exposed, the training, competence, and discipline of solicitors are regarded as of vital concern to the state, and this branch of the profession has, for some two hundred years, been rigorously controlled by the state under Solicitors Acts, although the exercise of the control has increasingly been delegated to the solicitors' professional body, the Law Society. The training of a solicitor involves compulsory law school attendance, the passing of a number of difficult examinations, and a period of apprenticeship (called "articles of clerkship") with a practising solicitor. The period of articles is five years in the case of those who have not taken a university law degree and two and a half years in the case of those who have. The minimum period of training is, therefore, five years. In the running of his practice the solicitor is

1 For a fuller description, see Brian Abel-Smith and R. B. Stevens, *Lawyers and the Courts* (London, 1967), and for a comparison with the American profession, see L. C. B. Gower and J. L. Price, "The Profession and Practice of the Law in England and America" (1957) 20 *Modern Law Review*, 317.

subject to stringent regulations regarding his charges, the accounts that he must keep, and the separation of his clients' money from his own. He must take out an annual practising certificate and contribute to an indemnity fund run by the Law Society.

Barristers, on the other hand, constitute a small corps of specialists; they are specialists primarily in advocacy but often also in particular branches of the law. There are only about 2,000 of them in full-time practice in England and they are concentrated in the major cities, especially London. They are not allowed to practise in partnership, either with other barristers or, *a fortiori*, with solicitors. They do, however, share sets of chambers, each set having a minimal office organisation. They are wholly free from state control, but they have their own self-regulating professional bodies—the ancient Inns of Court and the more modern General Council of the Bar.

Qualification is by joining an Inn, "keeping terms" (which now merely means eating a certain number of dinners), and passing examinations which are very much easier than those of the solicitors' branch. These examinations are run by the Council of Legal Education (a body sponsored by the Inns jointly) which also operates a school of law giving instruction on the subjects of the examination. Attendance at this school is optional. The whole process need take only two years[2] and can be, and often is, combined with study for a degree in law or some other discipline at a university. When it is completed the student is called to the bar by his Inn and is a fully fledged barrister-at-law. Until 1959 he could then practise in England and anywhere else where the qualification was recognised. It was traditional, how-

2 It was reduced from three years to two on June 1, 1965.

ever, for those who intended to practise to "read in chambers" by becoming pupils of a practising barrister. Recently an increasing number tried to save time and money by dispensing with this. The Inns of Court were rightly alarmed at this tendency, but were reluctant to make call to the bar more stringent since they are still imbued with the mediaeval view of the Inns as a kind of university where young men can go to acquire the education befitting a gentleman. They therefore insisted, instead, on an undertaking that a barrister, although "called," would not actually practise in England until he had undergone a year's pupillage. "Call" itself was made no more difficult and remains the easiest and cheapest of all professional qualifications.

I have described the system prevailing in England. In Scotland and Ireland it differs in detail but basically is the same. As will be seen, it is very much easier and quicker to qualify as a barrister rather than as a solicitor. It is also considerably cheaper unless the would-be solicitor can secure a living wage during the period of articles. Until quite recently this was unheard of, and, indeed, it was normal for him (or his parents) to pay a premium which might amount to as much as 500 guineas (say $1500) for the privilege of being apprenticed. Today premiums are very uncommon and a small salary, rarely amounting to a living wage, may be paid.

The relevance of all this to the African countries is this: up to the time of independence the primary qualification for enrolment as a legal practitioner in the fused professions was call to the bar or admission as a solicitor in England, Scotland, or Ireland. In West Africa this was indeed the sole qualification. In East Africa the legal qualifications of other Commonwealth countries were also recognised, but this was unimportant so far as African lawyers were concerned; in practice they did not go anywhere except to the British Isles. Nor, indeed, did many of them go there either, for there were virtually no African lawyers in East Africa.

In West Africa, however, there were, at independence, a considerable number—about eight hundred in Nigeria, two to three hundred in Ghana, and about eighty in Sierra Leone. With hardly an exception all of these had obtained their qualification by call to the English bar. The reason for this is obvious and not one for which they can be blamed. It was a grave strain on those who financed their training to send them to Britain at all. Naturally they chose the method which was the easier, quicker, and cheaper of the two.

In England a man is not considered to have received an adequate training for practice in the smaller branch of the profession there unless he has read both for a law degree and for the bar and subsequently had a year's pupillage in a good set of chambers. In Africa he was allowed to undertake the work of both branches of the profession without either a law degree or pupillage. His sole qualification might be (and usually was) call to the English bar. Even if supplemented by attendance at the three month's post-final course, now offered by the Inns of Court Law School, this was totally inadequate. In some respects, indeed, call to the bar was becoming more inadequate rather than less. Before the Second World War there had been only a trickle of students from overseas and they undoubtedly obtained some benefit from the close-knit collegiate atmosphere of the Inns and from the dining and lunching contacts with senior members of the English profession. After the war they came in floods and far outnumbered the English students. The facilities of the Inns and of the Inns of Court Law School were inadequate to cope with these numbers; some Inns indeed had to allow students merely to sign a book instead of sitting down to dinner —the *reductio ad absurdum* of "keeping terms." This decay of the collegiate atmosphere is one which senior African lawyers often fail to comprehend. They look back, through spectacles rose-tinted by time, to their own student days, and to the agreeable and instructive social contacts which they made, and are hurt and incredulous when their juniors denounce the so-called training as a painful and pointless farce.

Some African students, of course, fared rather better. They were the few who managed to secure a place at a British or Irish university so that they could read for a law degree. They at least acquired a more thorough and less didactic legal education and, if the university was residential, enjoyed a true collegiate atmosphere. But less than 25 per cent managed to gain admission to universities. And even the chosen few acquired an education primarily in English law and not at all in the laws of West or East Africa. In later years some of the African governments woke up to the need for lawyers with a solicitor's training and awarded scholarships for this purpose. But the African students found it difficult to obtain suitable articles. Partly, I fear, this was due to colour prejudice, concealed of course by the perennial excuse: "Nobody could be more liberal than I am, but my clients wouldn't like it." Partly it was due to the acute shortage of office accommodation and to an understandable wish to give priority to recruits who would stay after admission.

The failure of the English legal profession to do more

for African students constitutes to my mind one of the gravest indictments that can be levelled against us. Ever since the war, African bar students in England have outnumbered English students by about four to one. At any one time there have been in London about 2,000 African law students some of whom would undoubtedly be the future leaders of their countries. Had the Inns of Court faced up to this challenge, instituted courses suitable for future practitioners in Africa, and provided residential accommodation for colonial students, not only might the Inns of Court have become again the great educational institutions that they were in the Middle Ages but bonds of goodwill might have been forged which could have affected the whole history of the Commonwealth and of the common law. Instead, they did nothing until it was too late. All too many of the overseas students returned disgruntled and bearing ill-will. All returned inadequately equipped for their future roles.

In 1960 the Lord Chancellor appointed a committee under the chairmanship of Lord Denning to report on the position. Its main recommendations were that in future the African countries should not admit to local practice merely on the basis of British qualifications but should require additional practical training in the local law and procedure.[3] As we shall see, this advice has been heeded. It also suggested that the bar's post-admission course (which in practice was attended only by overseas students) should be extended in conjunction with the Law Society so as to include training in the solicitors' side of legal work, and that the Inns of Court Law School should be housed in more adequate prem-

3 *Report of the Committee on Legal Education for Students from Africa*, Cmd. 1255 of 1961.

ises. These latter suggestions also have borne some fruit.[4] But the new developments in England have been largely overtaken by events in Africa and I need not say more about them. Once again we did too little and too late.

In describing the effect of this legacy on the legal professions of the African territories at independence, I must deal separately with West and East Africa for the situation in each was very different. It differed not because of any difference in colonial policy regarding the production of indigenous lawyers. Everywhere, the officers of the colonial regime viewed the prospect of legally trained Africans with misgivings, regarding them, with some justification perhaps, as particularly likely to form an effective spearhead of the nationalist movements. Hence in neither West nor East Africa during the colonial era was any provision made for local legal training.

In West Africa, however, more advanced educational facilities were producing a stream of school-leavers with a passion for professional status, and, as I have pointed out, if money could be found for a spell in Britain, a barrister's qualification was the easiest professional qualification to attain. Many managed to raise the needed finance and when they returned were able to set up in practice without widespread expatriate competition. In East Africa, on the other hand, few Africans attained the needed educational qualifications and fewer still could find the money for an extended stay in Britain. Moreover the legal field had been largely pre-empted by settlers from Britain or the Indian subcontinent. Hence, as we shall see, the problem in West Africa was not so much that there were too few lawyers but rather that

[4] The main achievement has been infinitely better premises for the Inns of Court Law School.

there were too few good ones with a really thorough training for their public and professional roles. On the other hand, in East Africa (as in Central and Southern Africa) there were hardly any African lawyers at all.

In the West African countries there were, as I have already pointed out, considerable numbers of African lawyers. Since there were no local law schools, nearly all of these received their training as barristers in Britain.[5] It was as barristers that they thought of themselves and they tried to model their practices on those of their British brethren. There were few, if any, true partnerships, partly because Africans seem to find partnerships uncongenial and partly because they are contrary to the traditions of the British bar. However, as in Britain, there was often a sharing of accommodation and secretarial assistance which was even more attenuated than in the British model. They thought of the job of a lawyer as litigation, as barristers tend to do, but unlike their British brethren rarely regarded it as their duty to encourage settlement out of court. They were unevenly distributed—there were virtually none in the Muslim north—and were concentrated in the major cities, so that nowhere was there anything comparable to the English country-solicitor bringing legal advice to the doorstep of everyone.

Their ambitions, like those of most British barristers, were a political career or the bench which, at independence, was fast becoming Africanised. Many thought that the best route was via government service but most

[5] Some instruction for the first part of the English bar examination (which can be taken overseas) was provided at the Institute of Administration in Zaria and at the various branches of the Nigerian College of Arts and Science. Students who were successful in passing Part I had to go to England to complete the training. The Institute of Administration also provided training for native court judges.

wanted to serve as advocates (Crown Counsel, later State Counsel), not as legal advisers or draftsmen. They even adopted the distinctive rank of Queen's Counsel, a distinction which (*pace,* our Canadian friends) makes little sense in a fused profession, and which became totally inappropriate when their countries became republics.

The numerous indigenous lawyers were supplemented by a handful of British expatriates many of whom practised as solicitors and thereby monopolised most of the commercial work, especially that of expatriate business.[6] In the absence of any local specialists it was not uncommon for opinions to be sought from British barristers practising in London, and in litigation of any magnitude they were often brought from England to argue the case; all they had to do to be eligible to appear was to pay a fee and become enrolled.

One therefore had the ludicrous position that the lawyers in these countries received no formal training at all in their local law and practice. This, however, was perhaps the lesser of the two major absurdities; an intelligent and diligent lawyer would in time pick up a knowledge of these as he went along—though admittedly at the cost of his early clients. More ludicrous still was the fact that they had had no training at all in how to conduct the affairs and offer the services of a lawyer to whom a lay client had direct access. Whereas in England there were about 26,000 practising lawyers of whom about 2,000 were barristers, in West Africa there were about 1,100 lawyers in all, and all of them were barristers.

It would be overstating their qualifications even to

6 The largest and oldest established of these firms has branches in a number of Nigerian centres. The nearest equivalent in Ghana ceased practice in 1963.

say that they were fully equipped as trial lawyers. For the British barrister, whose training they had shared and whose outlook they imbibed, is not a fully equipped trial lawyer in your sense of that term. Litigation, if not handled solely by the solicitor as it can be in the lower courts, is a combined operation of barrister and solicitor. The barrister settles the pleadings, advises on evidence and conducts the case in court. The solicitor does the rest of the vitally essential preparation. He interviews the witnesses, takes their proofs of evidence, and prepares a detailed brief for the barrister. Hence the West African lawyer, though often a naturally endowed orator, was generally not particularly effective even as an advocate; he went into the forensic battle with one hand tied behind his back since the essential preparation, on which alone good advocacy can build, had not been done.

I have heard it argued that this did not really matter; that in our "adversary" system of litigation so long as the champions of both sides are equally handicapped justice will be done. I do not find this convincing. Justice according to law, even under the adversary system, surely demands that something approximating to the true facts should emerge at the trial, and that the judge should have his attention drawn to all the relevant legal authorities. A glance through the West African law reports will soon convince you that often neither was accomplished. Moreover, it did not follow that both sides would be equally handicapped. There were some exceptions to the general rule—brilliant and conscientious lawyers who had learned how to do their homework and did it.

If things were bad in the field of litigation they were far worse in non-litigious business in which most African lawyers were not only untrained but uninterested. Much legal drafting was incompetent and standards of conveyancing were abysmal. In most cases there was no attempt to follow the traditional course of agreeing a written contract, adducing and investigating title, agreeing the terms of a conveyance, and finally completion. The lawyer of the proposed vendor simply handed over to the would-be purchaser any deeds and documents the vendor had, and the purchaser's lawyer did the best he could. There was no control of professional conduct except a somewhat nebulous supervision exercisable by the courts. Few lawyers kept any proper books or attempted to separate their clients' money from their own. Some ran their practices on money obtained from or on behalf of their clients and hoped to be able to stave off the claims of one client until they had been put in funds by another.

Almost equally unsatisfactory was the fact that the client would find that his lawyer was not available for long stretches at a time. The lawyers were concentrated geographically to a far greater extent than the courts; if the lawyer had a case in a remote town he went off to argue it. Moreover, he needed a holiday occasionally. While he was away there was no one to whom the job could be delegated. Consequently it did not get done until he returned, if then. If in the meantime the client wanted a consultation he had to go on wanting.

To all this, as I have said, there were exceptions. Some of the few expatriate firms of solicitors strove to conduct their practices much as they would at home. Some Africans, too, achieved outstandingly high standards, especially as advocates and consultants and later as judges. But few if any had succeeded in establishing the office organisation and the partnerships which were needed if the lay client was to be assured of a constant and expert service. It was this, rather than prejudice, which caused expatriate businesses to take their legal work to the few expatriate law firms who could give them the service to which they were accustomed. But few African lawyers were prepared to recognise that that was the reason or, indeed, to recognise that general professional standards were low. Fewer still were prepared to recognise that the bar was ill-equipped to help with the major tasks of law reform that lay ahead. Happily, sufficient numbers of them did realise their own deficiencies (or at any rate the deficiencies of their colleagues) to lead to pressure for reform, and independence made some reforms essential. Countries which had thrown off the colonial yoke were not going to allow a situation to continue in which members of their prestige profession had to go to Britain to obtain their professional qualification, and in which the former colonial power decided who should be allowed to practise in their countries.

When one turns from West to East Africa one finds a very different but equally disturbing situation. There the legal profession was, and is still, almost exclusively non-African—British, Indian, and Pakistani. As in West Africa, professional standards were not all they might be, either as regards competence or ethics. But the professional bodies, and especially the Kenya Law Society, were more effective than any such body in West Africa. Moreover the fact that the profession had been dominated by expatriates had one important and encouraging consequence; there were far more office lawyers and genuine partnerships than in West Africa; the profession tended to think of itself as a body of solicitors rather than advocates alone.

The two great problems in East Africa were, therefore, first the absence of indigenous lawyers, and second, the absence of local facilities for training. The latter problem was the same as that faced by West Africa; the former was unique. In 1961, out of over three hundred qualified lawyers in Kenya, under ten were African; out of about one hundred and fifty in Uganda only twenty were African; out of about one hundred in Tanganyika, only one was African.[7] And virtually all of these few African lawyers were engaged in political activities or government service and were not in private practice. Private practice of law was monopolised by British and Asians who had qualified either in Britain or in the Indian subcontinent where, alas, the law school standards are generally depressingly low.[8] The only facilities for training locally were at a law school at Entebbe, Uganda, which was based on the model of the Institute of Administration, Zaria, and which since 1961 gave instruction to native court judges and students reading for Part I of the English bar examinations.[9]

2. *Post-Independence Developments*

One of the first acts of newly independent Ghana and Nigeria was to introduce legislation, derived from the English Solicitors Acts, designed to subject their legal professions to effective disciplinary control and, at the same time, to start local training schemes. In 1958

7 See the Denning Report, Cmnd. 1255, para. 6.

8 This is not intended to imply that the professional standards of Asian lawyers were necessarily lower than those of the British; in fact some are among the best.

9 The Zaria model was later followed in Nyasaland (Malawi) and Northern Rhodesia (Zambia).

Ghana passed the Legal Practitioners Act,[10] setting up a General Legal Council as the governing body of the profession, and started a crash programme for the local training of lawyers at the Accra Law School. In 1959 advisory committees in both Ghana and Nigeria produced broadly similar blueprints for future training and qualification in these countries.[11] Since these blueprints have been influential in setting the pattern for developments throughout anglophonic Africa, it may be worthwhile to say a few words about them.

In both cases the recommended method of training was a law degree at a university followed by one year's training in professional skills at a separate law school, controlled by the professional bodies. It was envisaged that both the university and the professional training would be available locally but that some recognition would be given to the degrees of overseas universities. After a transitional period British qualifications would no longer secure admission to the local bar.

Three questions arise in relation to these recommendations. The first concerns the length of the training. The Ghana committee reluctantly rejected the American solution of teaching law as a postgraduate discipline but felt that it was essential that the degree course

10 No. 22 of 1958. This was replaced in 1960 by the Legal Profession Act, Act No. 32.

11 In Ghana the committee was an international one consisting of Professor Arthur Sutherland of the Harvard Law School, Professor Zelman Cowen, Dean of the Faculty of Law, University of Melbourne, Australia, and myself, with Professor J. H. A. Lang, the first dean of the local faculty and Director of Legal Education (i.e., head of the Accra Law School). Its report was not printed but was distributed fairly widely in mimeographed form. In Nigeria the committee was comprised of local lawyers but it visited a number of other countries. Its report, *The Future of the Nigerian Legal Profession* (Lagos: Government Printer, 1959), is commonly known as the Unsworth Report after its chairman, Sir Edgar Unsworth, then the federal attorney general.

should include non-legal subjects and should take a minimum of four years. A similar recommendation would, I believe, have been practical politics in Nigeria also, but most unfortunately the Nigerian committee recommended three years merely.

Second, why no provision for articles or pupillage on the English model? The answer is that it was recognised that apprenticeship could not hope to work satisfactorily under local conditions. Indeed, we were dubious about whether it could ever work as well as properly organised institutional training.

Third, a question which Americans always ask, why the separation between the university faculty of law and the professional law school? In the case of Ghana one of the reasons was that the committee was faced with an existing situation—the Accra Law School was already functioning as a non-university institution. In the case of Nigeria one reason, which may or may not have been in the minds of the committee at the time but which later experience has thrown up, was inter-regional and regional-federal rivalries, which made an institution operated by a joint regional-federal Council of Legal Education more acceptable to the regions than a purely federal university. In both cases, undoubtedly, there was a desire on the part of the universities to avoid the risk of excessive pressure from the profession. And, speaking for myself, I believe that such a division has advantages. Though fully alive to the absurdity of seeking to draw a distinction between academic and practical subjects, I think there is an essential difference between the teaching of basic legal principles and techniques, and instruction into the "know-how" of professional practice. Students can profit from the former even though they do not intend to practise as lawyers; and Africa needs administrators and businessmen with that sort of training.[12] Legal practitioners need it too; but they also need further training in professional skills. Those who teach them must themselves have had recent practical experience and they must teach by supervising the students while they do the sort of tasks which lawyers have to undertake—interviewing clients, drafting legal documents, arguing cases, etc. Clearly the university could undertake this type of training, but the role is unfamiliar to the traditional English-style university. Moreover, if the university is situated some distance from the legal and commercial centre a separate "downtown" institution may be a better location.

Ghana immediately followed the report of its committee by commencing LL.B. instruction at the University of Ghana. Unfortunately, the law faculty speedily became the storm centre of disputes between the C.P.P. government and the university.[13] The first (English) dean was forced to leave in 1962, and Professor Burnett Harvey, his American successor, and his American second-in-command, were deported early in 1964.[14] Prior to this Dean Harvey had persuaded the General Legal Council to agree to the closure of the Accra Law School and to the ending of the crash programme based on part-

12 But it must be admitted that experience suggests that in the early days nearly all those who choose to read law will have it in mind to practise either privately or in the government legal service.

13 A full account will be found in Dean Harvey's mimeographed report to the Staffing of African Institutes of Legal Education and Research (SAILER) Project, "The Development of Legal Education in Ghana" (1964). See also his *Law and Social Change in Ghana* (Princeton, 1966), chap. iv and appendix 1.

14 The latter was subsequently invited to return and did so for a few months. He then became a senior lecturer at the University of Lagos but left there too as a result of its crisis, to be invited back to Ghana as a presidential professor! He is now a professor at the University of Wisconsin.

time study there.[15] Under his scheme the whole period of legal study was undertaken at the university, which offered a three-year B.A. in law followed by a two-year LL.B. for those who wished to be admitted to practice. This, however, did not long survive his departure. The present arrangements, as in Nigeria, are for a total period of training of four years only—a three-year law degree followed by a one year practical pre-admission course. The whole of this is undertaken at the university but the final year is organised by the General Legal Council and the courses consist largely of lectures by part-time teachers.

In Nigeria, too, things have not worked out exactly as plotted on the original blueprint. It was not until the spring of 1961 that the federal government declared its intention to implement the 1959 proposals. By then Ibadan was not the only university; another, a regional one, had started at Nsukka and three more were envisaged—one for each of the other regions, and another, a federal university, in Lagos. The federal government stated that a law faculty would be located in Lagos, rather than Ibadan as originally envisaged, and asked the regional governments to refrain from unnecessary duplication and not to create law faculties at their universities.[16] Within a month Nsukka announced that it was going to have a law faculty and shortly afterwards the other regional universities announced that they were too. Later efforts to prevent this admittedly wasteful use of human and material resources proved abortive; al-

15 Its results had been disappointing. Although over three hundred students had enrolled, only nine qualified lawyers had been produced. For details of Dean Harvey's scheme, see his *Law and Social Change in Ghana*, Appendix I.

16 *Educational Development, 1961-70*, Sess. Paper No. 3 of 1961, para. 51.

though everybody agreed that probably one and certainly a maximum of two law faculties—one in the north and one in the south—was all that the country needed at first, each region was determined that it should have one of the two. Hence we ended up with four. On the other hand all the regions were prepared to concede that the final year's practical training should be centralised at the Nigerian Law School in Lagos—a considerable concession in view of northern suspicion of the "pagan" south. But that has meant that law is taught at five different places.

The Nigerian scheme was brought into operation in 1962 under the Legal Education Act and Legal Practitioners Act of that year.[17] These acts set up a General Council of the Bar exercising general supervisory and disciplinary powers over the profession, and a separate Council of Legal Education concerned with recognition of academic qualifications and the running of the professional Nigerian Law School. Unfortunately this legislation contained some lamentably anti-expatriate provisions which restricted future enrolment to Nigerian citizens and disbarred all non-Nigerians then on the roll unless they were ordinarily resident in Nigeria at the date when the Act came into force.[18] This has made it impossible for expatriate firms to recruit further expatriate partners or associates.[19]

17 Act No. 12 of 1962 and Act No. 33 of 1962.

18 Act No. 33 of 1962, s. 3 (1)(a) and (5). This latter provision has had little practical effect since the chief justice is empowered to admit a non-Nigerian lawyer to argue a particular case: s. 2 (3).

19 The circumstances in which this lamentable provision came to be passed are not without interest. Originally, provisions regarding professional education, admission, discipline, and control were all contained in a single Legal Practitioners Bill. This encountered strong opposition from the Nigeria Bar Association, many of whose members did not take kindly to being subject to the same type of regulation as

Nigeria, however, avoided the Ghanaian mistake of instituting a crash programme for the production of instant lawyers.[20] Accordingly, the Nigerian Law School has been able to concentrate from the beginning on the one role of providing adequate pre-admission training for those who have previously acquired an academic legal qualification either at a Nigerian university or overseas. In this it has already had some success despite the fact that until now most of its intake has been from those who have read for the bar in England and who, under transitional provisions which have now ended, needed to attend the school for three months only.[21] In

---

that provided under the Solicitors Acts. Accordingly it was decided to hive-off the provisions relating to legal training and qualification into a separate Legal Education Bill. This did not prove as non-controversial as had been hoped (see *Parliamentary Debates* [Senate], 1961-62, cols. 497-504) but was eventually enacted early in 1962.

The government was anxious to enact the regulatory provisions of the Legal Practitioners Bill, but the Foot and Gratiaen incidents (see chap. ii above) put them in a weak position to resist the inclusion of provisions protecting Nigerian practitioners against expatriate competition. One might have thought that these provisions go far enough (to put it mildly), but agitation still continues in favour of further restriction on the few remaining expatriate practitioners. It is quite impossible to convince most Nigerian lawyers that expatriate firms get a disproportionate amount of the lucrative work not because of unfair practices or prejudice but because of superior organisation. None of the other African countries has equivalent anti-expatriate provisions. In Ghana, for example, non-Ghanaians can still qualify so long as they comply with the same training requirements as Ghanaians (Legal Profession Act, 1960 (Act No. 32), s. 3(1); contrast Act No. 22 of 1958, s. 4 which restricted admission to Ghanaians); those already enrolled were not disbarred.

20 The nearest approach was the scheme sponsored by the Northern Nigerian government whereby students read for Part I of the English bar examination at the Institute of Administration, Zaria, and were then sent to England to read for Part II (see n. 5 *supra*).

21 Until 1965 Nigeria, unlike Ghana, continued to recognise call to the British bar as partial fulfilment of its requirements. When the period of keeping terms was reduced to two years, Nigeria decided not to recognise call to the bar unless supported by a university degree—not necessarily in law.

Ghana the pre-admission courses have only recently been brought into operation and have not yet succeeded in providing quite the same experience of learning by doing as has already been instituted in Nigeria. Nigeria has also met the need for part-time instruction by instituting evening schools for the LL.B. degrees of Lagos University and the University of Ife at Ibadan.[22]

Although no law teacher in Nigeria has actually shared Professor Harvey's experience of deportation, Nigeria's universities and law school have unfortunately not been much more successful than other Nigerian institutions in escaping from the influence of tribal politics and from the interference with academic freedom and harmony which that entails. However, the results of tribalism may be said to have justified the proliferation of law schools, for students are now unwilling to go to a university outside their own region. Indeed, the concentration of post-graduate professional training at the Nigerian Law School in Lagos has broken down, at least temporarily; the Ibo students have fled from it and a second professional school has been improvised for them in Enugu. If this becomes a permanent establishment the last unifying element in Nigerian legal education will have been destroyed.

Neither Sierra Leone nor the Gambia yet has any local scheme of legal training in operation. In view of the Gambia's minute size and population it is difficult to see how she could ever support her own law school. The most she could hope to do is to follow the example of the former High Commission Territories of Basutoland,

22 At Lagos a minimum of five years is prescribed; at Ife four. It is perhaps too early yet to say how successful these evening schools will prove to be but the demand for places is heavy and the wastage less than had been feared.

Bechuanaland and Swaziland of a joint programme with a university in another country.[23] Sierra Leone, however, is about to introduce a local scheme based upon a report of a committee which met there in February, 1965.[24] Their plan represents what could be an improvement on those of either Ghana or Nigeria. The university (Fourah Bay University College) will provide training for a four-year LL.B., accepting entrants with ordinary level General Certificates of Education (instead of the advanced level normally prescribed for university entry), and for a further year's practical instruction for those who wish to qualify for practice. In other words the total period of training will be five years instead of only four, which I am sure is inadequate even with the slightly higher entry requirements prescribed in Ghana and Nigeria. The whole of this training, as now in Ghana, will be undertaken at a university, but the committee emphasise that the final year's instruction should be based on practical tasks on the lines attempted at the Nigerian Law School. They particularly stress the need to associate a legal aid clinic with this training, as has been done in Nigeria.

In East Africa the first step towards reform was taken by Julius Nyerere even before independence.[25] He be-

23 There the local university at Roma provides instruction during the preliminary and final years, and Edinburgh University (selected because of the civil law background of southern Africa) during the two intermediate years. Such an arrangement is economical in terms of local staff and has many advantages, especially if, as would be possible with common law jurisdictions, the arrangement could be with another African university.

24 The overseas advisers on this committee were Dean A. B. Weston of Dar es Salaam, Professor Thomas Franck of New York University, and myself.

25 For a fuller account of developments in East Africa, see the admirable article by W. L. Twining, "Legal Education Within East Africa," in *East African Law Today* (British Institute of International

lieved that the paucity of African lawyers posed such a grave problem for Tanganyika that he was not prepared to postpone local training until the proposed branch of the University of East Africa was built at Dar es Salaam. But he and his advisers resisted the temptation to introduce a crash programme for the production of lawyers with inferior qualifications. Instead, temporary premises, the new TANU headquarters, were made available and there the university college started in October, 1961 with one faculty—law—providing a three-year LL.B. This faculty made a splendid start and a remarkably trouble-free one when compared with the West African experience, though it has very recently had some difficulties with its students.

The overall position of legal training in East Africa is, however, somewhat confused. Although all three territories have, since independence, amended their Advocates Ordinances, there are considerable differences between Kenya on the one hand, and Uganda and Tanganyika on the other.[26] And in none does the legislation reflect the actual position very faithfully. The original intention had been that the university college at Dar should provide the initial academic training for all three territories, but that, as in West Africa, this would be supplemented by subsequent pre-admission training at a professional law school.[27] Kenya has in fact set up such a school in Nairobi. But the Kenya Law Society retains an old-fashioned predilection for articles of

---

and Comparative Law, Commonwealth Law Series No. 5; London, 1966), pp. 115-51.

26 (Kenya) Advocates Act, 1961 (Cap 16 of 1962 Revision); (Tanganyika) Act No. 16 of 1963; (Uganda) Acts No. 55 and 59 of 1963.

27 The Denning Committee thought that one only would suffice at first, and it was envisaged that this would be in Nairobi. See Cmnd. 1255, para. 62.

clerkship as a method of training and has secured that apprenticeship, supplemented by courses at the law school, shall be one of the methods of qualifying in Kenya. Until now the role in fact performed by the Nairobi Law School has been to provide these courses for articled clerks—originally on a part-time basis but latterly by full-time "sandwich" courses.

This method of qualifying is not recognised in Uganda or Tanganyika. Their method is either through admission in another Commonwealth country, or through an approved university law degree (normally at Dar). These alternatives are also recognised by Kenya, except that the only overseas admission now recognised there is British.[28] Whichever alternative is adopted, a pre-admission period of local practical training is prescribed, but no institutional arrangements for it have yet been made. The net result is that Kenyan Africans qualify either through articles, or through a law degree at Dar followed by a short period of in-training, while Ugandans and Tanzanians do so only through the law degree followed by such in-training. The Kenyan articled clerks do not receive what most legal educators would regard as an adequate basis of theory and, according to the quality of the firms to whom they are articled, may or may not receive proper practical instruction; the rest receive a sound academic training but are not given any real practical training at all before they are admitted.[29]

28 The practical result is that Indian and Pakistani qualifications are no longer recognised in Kenya, whereas they still are in Uganda and Tanganyika.

29 The faculty at Dar have done their best to meet this need by attaching their incoming students to magistrates and the like during the seven month gap between the time when they leave school and enter the university. They have also found legal vacation jobs for many of their students.

The whole position is, however, very fluid. There is some talk of both Kenya and Uganda introducing law degrees at their own branches of the University of East Africa, which like most of the former common services, seems to be breaking up into its component parts. Kenya already has a small law department at the university college in Nairobi[80] which could form the nucleus of a faculty in due course if two separate law schools there are thought to be essential.

It is generally said that the problems of East Africa in the building up of a legal profession are far more serious than those of West Africa. In the short run that is undoubtedly true. The new African rulers will not for much longer allow the legal profession to be dominated by British and Asian practitioners; significant moves here have been the recruitment of Nigerians and Ghanaians as judges, magistrates, and parliamentary counsel. As in West Africa, the days of the expatriate lawyer are clearly numbered. Less clear is the position of the not inconsiderable number of non-African (mainly Asian) lawyers who have taken out citizenship. If they are allowed to remain and are gradually supplemented by Africans, the long-term position may well be more favourable than in West Africa. East Africa at least starts with a relatively clean slate. She does not have the problem of a large body of practitioners who think that the main job of a lawyer is to litigate. If the change to an Africanised profession can be made without too grave a lowering of standards during the transitional period, if the solicitor-type tradition which the expatriate firms have established can be maintained and built on, East Africa in twenty years time could well

80 At present it provides some legal instruction for students of other faculties.

have a healthier legal profession than West Africa. One dangerous tendency at the moment, however, is that nearly all the Africans are joining the public legal service, leaving private practice to the Asians. A racial division between the public and the private sectors is not healthy.

The urgent task, as I see it, is to supplement the academic training at Dar with proper practical training. The penchant for articles of clerkship displayed by the Kenya Law Society is, I am sure, a calamity. The English Law Society now realises that apprenticeship only works if articled clerks can be placed in good offices where they will be assured of proper training. The embarrassing task of "approving" certain firms and banning others has been rejected as impracticable. That task would be even more embarrassing in Africa, where it would inevitably become entwined with considerations of race and colour. Yet it is clear that in Africa many lawyers' offices are worse than any in England. Everywhere else the movement is away from apprenticeship toward law school training, and the sooner all East Africa joins the movement the better for the future of its legal profession.

Despite local variations a common pattern of legal training seems to be emerging throughout anglophonic Africa.[31] The favoured method is via a university law

31 I have not, in this lecture, dealt with other parts of anglophonic Africa where local law-teaching is in operation. These include the Sudan (where law-teaching in the University of Khartoum started in 1936), Liberia (where the Louis Arthur Grimes School of Law was founded in 1954), Ethiopia (where the Law School of the Haile Selassie I University was established in 1963 with Professor James Paul of the Pennsylvania Law School as the first dean), Basutoland (Lesotho, where the university at Roma started legal instruction in 1965), Rhodesia (where a law degree course was instituted in the same year), and Zambia (where such a course started in 1966).

degree followed by practical training at a professional law school, which may or may not be associated with the university. Not only does the training take place locally, it is designed to fit recruits for local practice and not, as in the former French territories, to lead to a *license en droit* identical with that of the former colonial power. It has been recognised that this training must include subjects such as international law, business corporations, and commercial law, which will become increasingly important as these countries develop commercially and increase their association with other African countries. It is accepted that every effort should be made to ensure that lawyers have some degree of sophistication in non-legal disciplines such as economics and political science,[82] and that they have a sufficient knowledge of French to be able to communicate with lawyers in the French-speaking territories that surround them. It is also recognised that the lawyers needed are those who will look critically at the law and the organisation of the legal profession.

Every effort is being made to ensure that the proliferation of universities does not lead to a lowering of standards such as has occurred in some Asian countries. To this end all the law faculties are determined to continue to associate external examiners with their degree examinations. This practice, is of course, unknown in the United States but I am sure that it is absolutely essential under African conditions. It does not prevent the teacher

82 A most useful development here has been the annual seminars on "Law and Economic Development" held at the University College, Dar es Salaam, under the chairmanship of Professor Wolfgang Friedmann of the Columbia University Law School, and attended by lawyers, civil servants, and law students from East and Central Africa. The difficulty is to find room for the non-legal disciplines in a three-year curriculum, but an extension of the teaching year has helped.

from having primary responsibility for examining his students but it does enable him to have the help and advice of an experienced, internationally known, outside expert in the setting of the paper and the marking of the scripts, and ensures that proper standards are maintained.[33]

Many problems remain to be solved: What is the ideal curriculum? What the most appropriate teaching method? Here the proliferation of law schools and the diversity of teachers—drawn as they are at present from Africa, Britain, and America—are positive advantages. Each law school can learn from the experiments of others—the English-trained teacher from his American colleague's use of the casebook method and the American-trained teacher from his English colleague's use of the tutorial system. Texts and casebooks on African law are sorely needed but are now being produced in both quantity and quality. Building up the requisite law libraries is another formidable task but one upon which an excellent start has been made.

Basic academic training is at present in advance of practical training. Only Nigeria has yet made a real start with a professional law school where professional skills and proper standards can be instilled. And even in Nigeria it has still not made a serious impact on the profession or converted it from one that regards litiga-

33 Among the advantages of the system are: (1) it helps to achieve and maintain comparability of standards and international confidence in those standards—vitally important in the recruitment of staff and to students wishing to take postgraduate degrees abroad; (2) it helps to turn aside the wrath of failed students and thereby to preserve student-teacher harmony. Students who fail examinations tend to blame anyone but themselves, and the normal targets for their resentment are the teachers. This is especially so when tribal differences intrude. The external examiner provides the teacher with an alibi.

tion as its objective rather than its failure. Nor, in present circumstances, can its future be regarded as assured. Perhaps the gravest unsolved problem regarding technical competence is that of producing adequate numbers of skilled legal draftsmen. Drafting, whether of legislation or of wills, conveyances, or agreements, is a difficult enough task even if the draftsman can use his first language. The difficulties are the greater when, as in Africa, the indigenous draftsman must use a language which he probably did not learn until he went to school and which he may then have been taught indifferently. To this day even Ghana and Nigeria still find it necessary to recruit expatriates as parliamentary counsel.

In addition to these problems there are more fundamental questions to which as yet little or no consideration has been given, but which are rightly asked by my colleague Professor Twining in a recent article.[34] In all the new training schemes the private practitioner of the Anglo-American type is taken as the production model. Is this realistic? In East Africa (and for that matter Central and Southern Africa) initially at any rate, new African recruits to the legal profession will not become private practitioners but will go into the magistracy or government service. So will many of those in West Africa. Do they need the same sort of training as private practitioners? The schemes recognise that administrative personnel may need no further training after the LL.B., the courses for which seek to meet their needs as well as those of practitioners. But magistrates, public prosecutors, state counsel, parliamentary draftsmen, and so on, clearly do need further training.[35] But do they

[34] *East African Law Today* (see n. 25 *supra*), pp. 139-44.

[35] An interesting experiment in providing this sort of training was the seven-month course in legal administration held in Jerusalem in 1965-6 and described in (1966) 1 *Israel Law Review*, 632-35.

need the same sort of training as those proposing to enrol as private practitioners? Is it correct to assume and encourage a mobility between the magistracy and government legal service on the one hand and private practice on the other?[36] Again, how does one ensure that the small reservoirs of well-educated manpower are not drained to provide an excessive number of private legal practitioners? Indeed, is private practice as we know it what these countries need—at any rate until they have solved the overwhelming problem of poverty, which is especially acute in East Africa?

At present over 90 per cent of their populations have real per capita incomes of under $120 per annum. Can a profession operating for private gain and with relatively high expectations of financial reward really meet this challenge? Everywhere lip-service is paid to the need for legal aid schemes; but little is done about it and, even if they were introduced, could schemes based on a private profession operating for reward cope with the problem? Should the profession be nationalised as so many services in these countries are nationalised? The answer may be no, because only an independent bar can be the bulwark of individual liberty. But is that answer going to appeal to nationalist leaders who regard the situation in their countries as an emergency akin to war, in which all resources must be channelled into a united effort? Can a private bar remain a bulwark without coming to be regarded, as it almost had in Ghana, as an obstacle to progress which must be swept away? Of all the legal institutions that I have known in recent years, that which impressed me most was one on the

36 The Colonial Legal Service kept its lawyers divorced from private practice and throughout most of the civilised world the magistracy is a separate career service.

opposite side of the world—the Public Solicitor of Papua and New Guinea. His organisation provides free legal assistance to all the local population that seek it and, as at present administered, it is certainly not less independent and courageous than the bar in Africa. If the British had bequeathed to Africa something like that, our legacy might have been more valuable. If there is anything at all in all these questions, may it not be that we are training a future legal profession for a form of practice that had no future? I hope not.

3. *The Needed Aid*

That brings me at long last to my final question: What can we in the West, and in particular, you in the United States do to help?

First, perhaps, is the question why should you help? To this I can think of only one adequate answer: because it is in your interest to do so. It is a trite observation that today the world is one and indivisible. Instability anywhere affects stability everywhere. Africa is already one of the storm-centres. If, as I hope I have convinced you, strong legal professions are needed in Africa to preserve stability there, I need say no more about why it is in your interest to do all you can to ensure that it has such professions.

A secondary, but emotionally potent, consideration is that all nations like to "make friends and influence people" and the United States particularly likes to be loved—it is one of your most endearing traits. At present you are not greatly loved in Africa. This is surprising. I find you a particularly lovable people and your relative freedom from the taint of colonialism should, one would have thought, have made you especially congenial to the African nations—certainly more congenial than the British. But the fact is that you are not, and this surprising fact has to be faced. The more you help, the more your image may be improved. But please do not expect that your help will be accepted with greater eagerness than help from Britain or with much greater eagerness than help from Russia or China. Your great advantage over us is that you have more help to offer; your great advantage over the East is that anglophonic, common law Africa finds you easier to understand.

If this secondary motive is dominant please do your best to conceal it. The Peace Corps was launched with the tremendous handicap that its very name proclaimed it to be a weapon in the Cold War. That it has surmounted that handicap (for unquestionably the Peace Corps is one of the world's greatest success stories) is a tribute to the admirable young men and women who have done so much for the developing nations and who, incidentally, have exemplified America and Americans at their best. They have undoubtedly made many Americans as individuals deeply loved in Africa. But I do not think that they have materially enhanced the influence of the United States as such, or persuaded the African nations of the virtues of the American capitalist system or way of life. I do not believe that aid can do that, any more than I believe that Russian or Chinese aid can have much effect in the opposite direction.

Again, do not expect or ask for gratitude. I mention this because I was told that the representative of one of your major foundations exclaimed in a moment of exasperation with Ghana: "How can these people expect us to help them if they don't show a bit of gratitude." If he said that, it was, uncharacteristically, a foolish remark. The African rulers are realists. They realise that if you help it is because you think it in your interest to do so. With memories of the slave trade and of colonialism they think you owe them a debt anyway. They will probably say "thank you"; partly because they are polite people, partly because they realise that this is tactful if they hope for more. But they will not feel gratitude. Why on earth should they? But they will feel resentment if help is refused. Again I quote Frank Sutton: "They expect and will need further help about which they will often have to be gracelessly demanding. Guiding hands will have to be light, deft and inconspicuous to be acceptable. But their absence will be resented and their ultimate effects not trivial."[37]

What then is the help that should be given? In relation to legal training a great deal is already being done in three principal ways; and what, I think, is needed is to maintain and, if possible, to increase this assistance.

1. This first way in which help is being given is in financial support of specific projects by the great American foundations. Already there are a number of projects for which foundation help has been sought. One is the institution in Nigeria of a scheme for continuing legal education for the bar. Another is for the establishment in Africa of an institute of advanced research into African law. In the exploratory stages of both, the Ford Foundation has already been most helpful. The third is the organisation of conferences of teachers from the various law schools of Africa—very desirable if the isolation of East from West Africa and of anglophonic

[37] In Tilman and Cole (eds.), *The Nigerian Political Scene*, p. 283. Unfortunately circumstances may arise, as they did in 1965 at the University of Lagos, where the "guiding hands" may find it impossible to act consistently with their principles and consciences and yet remain "inconspicuous."

from francophonic Africa is to be broken down. Here again the admirable Ford Foundation has helped, as has the Leverhulme Trust. A fourth project, in which some interest has already been expressed, is in instituting pilot schemes of legal aid for the indigent.[38]

Douglas Gustafson,[39] in a recent publication, ventured three criticisms of American aid to projects of this sort and these I should like humbly to echo. The first is of the "Me-Tell-You" attitude which has characterised too much foreign aid. Sometimes, as I know, foundations have given the impression that if they suggest a project and are prepared to back it, they think it wholly unreasonable for the African authorities to decline. This, as again I know, has given rise to resentment. As one vice-chancellor put it: "These chaps mustn't think they can buy me with their dollars." That may be thought merely another example of post-colonial hypersensitivity. But it must be remembered that foundations rarely agree to underwrite indefinitely the whole cost of any project; they merely "prime the pump" and no one wants to be left with a second-hand pump in what he thinks may prove to be a dry well.

The second criticism, which applies mainly, I think, to assistance from the Agency for International Development, is of the "Buy American" rule. This is of particular relevance to the equipment of law libraries. There is, of course, a need for books on American law and no one minds buying these from the United States. But

38 Reference has already been made to schemes for associating legal aid clinics with professional training at the law schools. At the Nigeria Law School, where such a clinic is already in operation, it has been but poorly patronised, possibly because the Nigerian public, unlike the English, is too proud to attend an institution described as a "poor man's lawyer centre."

39 *Managing Economic Development in Africa* (Cambridge, Mass., 1963), p. 222.

there is a far greater immediate need for books published in Britain and I do not have to tell you that these can be purchased very much more cheaply in Britain than in the States. It is frustrating to see one's lovely dollars go down the drain.

The third is of what Mr. Gustafson calls "Cook's Tours." He is especially critical of the amount spent to take influential Africans on short tours of the States. He says: "After talking with Africans who have been on these 'holidays' it is clear that (a) they appreciate the generosity of the United States for giving them the trip, but (b) they are no more pro-American than before going, and (c) for the amount of money spent, their country will benefit very little . . . . We are fooling ourselves if we attach a high degree of effectiveness to dollars spent in this fashion."[40] I emphatically agree; though it ill becomes me—at present enjoying a "Cook's Tour"—to say so.

There are also "reverse Cook's Tours" whereby "consultants" pay short visits to Africa to solve "vaguely defined problems."[41] Those who live in Africa get the impression, which I am sure is exaggerated, that at any one time about a hundred American V.I.P.s are swanning round Africa at enormous expense to report on the feasibility of half-baked propositions. Africans tend to feel that if half the amount spent on looking at what might be done had been spent on doing something, twice as much might have been accomplished. When the consultant brings an expertise to bear that no one on the spot could, then, of course, the money is well spent. But often one suspects that your local representatives (who are not exactly thin on the ground) could

40 *Ibid.*, p. 224.
41 See William L. Hooper, *ibid.*, p. 217.

give far better advice than any consultant who only spends a few days in the country.

I hope I do not underestimate the extent to which such visits are necessary in terms of American domestic politics, or to persuade those who control the purse-strings to untie them. In particular, I hope that none of you will think that visits from you are not welcome (they are). My plea is simply that those who send you on public or foundation money should ask themselves, in the words of Britain's wartime posters: "Is your journey really necessary?" Unnecessary journeys at public expense are not a good example to African leaders who are quite ready enough to go off with large entourages on Cook's Tours of their own.

2. The second way of helping is by making openings available to African students at the American law schools. So far as basic LL.B. training is concerned, my own view is that it is now a positive disservice for the United States to encourage, by scholarship grants or otherwise, Africans from the countries with which I am concerned to go to American law schools. Training is now available locally and, because it is directed towards local conditions, it is more relevant than any that can be obtained elsewhere. If you attract the best men and women you are merely depriving the African law schools of them and, because the development of secondary schools lags behind that of universities, some of these law schools are already having to scrape the bottom of the barrel in order to secure their quota of qualified students.

If you want to help with the basic training there are other ways of doing so. One would be to endow some scholarships or revolving loan funds at those African law schools where students are not financially supported by the state. In Nigeria, for example, law students rarely are—despite the shortage of legal draftsmen and despite the fact that the governments have insisted that law should be among the first faculties at all their universities! This short-sighted policy (as I think) means that the best students tend to choose subjects other than law. What Nigeria needs is an improvement in the quality rather than the quantity of her lawyers. Some scholarships would help to achieve that.[42]

But on the postgraduate level the American law schools have much to contribute. The new African law faculties cannot for some years embark on ambitious LL.M. programmes. What I would like to see is a small but steady stream of potential law teachers spending a year at good American law schools after taking their LL.B. in Africa. It is not necessary, and perhaps not even desirable, that the American law schools should institute courses in African law for this purpose. The students will already have been exposed to African law. What they need is exposure to American law teachers and American teaching methods. If in the process they learn some American law (especially constitutional law) so much the better. In the short-term too, there is a need for openings at those American law schools which specialise in African studies so that African scholars can undertake research into aspects of African law. Frankly, however, I regard this as a short-term need until institutes of legal research can be established in Africa. To my mind the place for research into African

[42] In 1964, for the first time, the federal government granted some scholarships for law—but only six out of 606 scholarships awarded. Still, this shows a (belated) recognition of the need. At the Nigerian Law School no scholarships are available, but scholarships awarded to law undergraduates have been continued during the final year at the Law School.

law is Africa, where alone the essential field work can be done.

Meeting these needs should not demand any increase in the present number of American scholarships and fellowships. African countries already have available to them more postgraduate awards than they can fill, and the quality of some of the recipients has left much to be desired.

3. America can, and is, helping with the staffing and equipment of the African law schools. The SAILER[43] Project, the Peace Corps, the Agency for International Development, the M.I.T. Fellows in Africa Program, the Syracuse Program, and the foundations have all contributed nobly. There are already more American law teachers in ex-British Africa than there are British, and without their assistance several of the law schools would never have got off the ground, or would have crashed after take-off. Despite some initial resistance to recruitment of Americans (an example of the suspicion of American methods strongly felt in educational and legal circles), they have, almost without exception, been conspicuously successful.[44] In only one respect has this

43 SAILER (Staffing of African Institutes of Legal Education and Research) is a project administered by the Institute of International Education and supported by the major American law schools.

44 One minor problem is that most American teachers want to teach constitutional law. This is not the subject in which the need is greatest, since most African teachers also want to teach it—their new constitutions naturally fascinate them. Since this is a sensitive area it is probably better, other things being equal, that teaching should be by an African rather than an expatriate. Moreover there is, I think, a tendency for American teachers to try to equate the new African constitutions with that of the United States. I was wont to tease my American colleagues by telling them that every American lawyer starts with an initial assumption that any written constitution is based on that of the United States; if he finds that it is a federal constitution his assumption is confirmed, and if it contains a bill of rights, too, he regards the presumption as irrebuttable. This, of course, is a gross

aid been inadequate; the teachers supplied have generally been young and inexperienced and few have been willing to stay long enough.

The great unmet need is for men with about ten years' teaching experience, who can bridge the gap in filling senior posts until the young African teachers acquire the requisite experience, and who will stay for a *minimum* of two years. They should, of course, be carefully selected. Beware of those dedicated "do-gooders" who are imbued with missionary zeal—a man who goes to dodge the draft or because he wants a change of environment, is a much safer bet. Do not assume that a coloured American will be especially acceptable; he too will be regarded as an "expatriate" and is likely (as many moving accounts by Negroes have revealed) to be subject to considerable emotional strains. Do not choose anyone who cannot reconcile himself to the absence of American standards of sanitation and hygiene (they do not exist anywhere else) or who will be shocked if invited to "see Africa." And pay particular attention to the wives who generally find more difficulty than their husbands in adjusting to the new environment.

In addition to supplying teachers the American law schools have been most generous in helping to equip the law libraries of the African law schools, most of which are, as a result, surprisingly good. But all the African law schools will continue to need and ask for more. And many countries are lamentably lacking in American material. It is said that outside the law library at

---

exaggeration but I think it contains a germ of truth. It is unnecessary to emphasise that, except in the most remote historical sense, none of the African constitutions (except those of Liberia and Ethiopia) owes anything (except federalism which is not proving very viable) to American ideas; it may well be that they would be better if they did.

the university college at Dar es Salaam, the only American law book in East Africa is one copy of Gray's Perpetuities.

In relation to aid to the universities may I, however, venture on one criticism? I am very unhappy about the type of assistance given when the Agency for International Development enters into a contract with an American university whereby the latter undertakes to be responsible for the running of an African university or one department of it. When this occurs the American university naturally considers that its reputation is at stake and seeks to control operations from its home base. This places the unfortunate teachers in the impossible position of trying to serve two masters—the home university and the African one—and the African authorities resent being tied to the American apronstrings. Paternalism of this sort is an anachronism in this part of Africa.[45] I am absolutely convinced that the only way to give help is to supply men and materials and leave the men to get on with the job as temporary servants of the African university. There is a risk, of course, that they will make a mess of it, but they are less likely to do so than those 4,000 miles away without detailed knowledge of local conditions. There is also a risk that if, as they should, they seek to maintain academic standards, they may get into hot water. And then it is the home university's role to be more understanding and helpful than a government agency or rep-

45 Yet there seems to be too little recognition of this in American circles. Cf. John W. Gardner's quite critical *A.I.D. and the Universities* (New York, 1964), which took the view that "the university man wants to feel (and act as though) he has the whole weight and dignity of his [American] institution behind him . . ." (p. 9), and obviously thought that he should be encouraged and helped to feel and act in that undesirable fashion.

resentative is likely to be. The latter will think that the teacher is "rocking the boat"—the unforgivable sin in their eyes. A university can afford to take the view that the important thing is to help to steer the boat in the right direction.

These, then, as I see it, are the three main ways in which the United States can help. Perhaps the greatest long-term gain to be expected from such help is in the production of an African legal profession with a livelier appreciation of the needs of tomorrow and of the defects of the institutions which we, the British, have bequeathed. We have stamped our mark on the law and on the lawyers of these countries. Whether we or they like it or not, the mark is probably indelible, but it can be reshaped without too drastic plastic surgery. The trouble is that most African lawyers like it as it is—that is the usual result of the didactic, uncritical, legal training that they have received in England. Yet if these countries are to respond to the challenges of the future it must be altered. If, for instruction by English lawyers at the Inns of Court, one merely substitutes instruction by English-trained lawyers at the African universities the change may not come about. There may be an improvement in technical competence for local practice; that would be something indeed, but not enough. It is because I want more to be achieved that I want more African lawyers to be exposed to American methods at American law schools, and more American teachers to practise American methods at African law schools.

I do not want American aid wholly to supersede British. I think Britain still has a contribution to make —if I did not I should not have gone to Africa. And I think that our respective contributions should be in combination and not in competition. On the technical level we can both contribute. Your unique contribution is to shake us, and African lawyers, out of complacency. And if, as I should like to think, you have not found these lectures *too* complacent, I can only remind you that when I was here twelve years ago some of you were wont to say to me, and I think you *intended* it as a compliment: "But of course you aren't a typical Englishman." I wouldn't know about that. But I think too many African lawyers are.

Index